Tastes
and
Tales
from Russia

By
Alla Danishevsky

PublishAmerica
Baltimore

First printing

ISBN: 1-4137-2320-9
PUBLISHED BY PUBLISHAMERICA, LLLP
www.publishamerica.com
Baltimore

Printed in the United States of America

This book is dedicated to my loving family.
To my husband for all of his help and support with this book. Thank you to Rochella and Tyler who let me work in peace to finish this project. Also, great thanks to my parents and in-laws for sharing their wisdom.

Table of Contents

Appetizers

Salad Vinaigrette

This is a light, healthy beet salad that can be served at parties, or enjoyed at the dinner table.

Serves 6

Ingredients:
3 potatoes
2 carrots
3 large beets
3 pickles
1 large onion
3 tablespoons sunflower or olive oil
Pepper, dill and parsley to taste

Method:
Boil potatoes, carrots and beets until soft. Cube boiled potatoes, beets, carrots and pickles. Chop onions. Combine all the ingredients. Season with sunflower oil and pepper.

Serving suggestion: Garnish the salad with dill and parsley. Serve chilled.

Tale of Ruslan and Ludmila

One of the most popular amongst Russian tales, Ruslan and Ludmila was written as poetry by the famous Alexander Pushkin.

Once upon a time, in an exotic far away land, there was a celebration taking place. It was the marriage of the land's greatest warrior, Ruslan, to the land's most beautiful maiden, Ludmila. During the celebration, the bride was kidnapped by the dwarf magician, Chernomor. Angry, Ludmila's father made an announcement to the kingdom that he would give his daughter's hand in marriage to the warrior who rescued her from Chernomor.

Ruslan and his rival warriors, Farlaf, Ratmir, and Rogdai, prepared to rescue the beautiful maiden. Ruslan knew that he would have to overcome great obstacles and magical powers to rescue his bride. Rogdai killed Ratmir, and then attacked Ruslan. But Ruslan won the fight, and threw Rogdai into the River Dnieper. Ruslan wandered farther into the unknown land where he entered a thick fog and came upon a giant magic head. Underneath the head was a knife, which he knew he must take in order to defeat Chernomor. Ruslan defeated the head and took the knife. He then used this knife to cut off the dwarf's beard, which held the dwarf's magical powers.

With Chernomor's powers gone, Ruslan was able to defeat him. Ruslan went to look for Ludmila and found his bride in a magical garden. He brought Ludmila back to the feast where they were finally married.

Salad Olivier

This is a cousin of Salad Vinaigrette, without the beets. They can be served and enjoyed at the same table.

Serves 8

Ingredients:
5 potatoes
3 carrots
4 eggs
1 package of hot dogs
1/2 pound green peas
3 dill pickles
Salt to taste
1/2 pound mayonnaise

Method:
Boil potatoes and carrots in skin, then cool them down and peel them. Boil eggs and boil hot dogs. Chop potatoes, carrots, eggs, hot dogs, dill pickles into 1/2 inch squares. Add green peas and salt. Stir in the mayonnaise. Mix the salad and refrigerate for awhile.

Serving suggestion: Garnish with parsley and cilantro.

Tale of Princess Swan

Long ago in a far away kingdom, Tsar Saltan sat listening to the future plans of three sisters. One of these sisters said that if the tsar was to marry her she would prepare a great feast for the entire kingdom. The second sister said that if she was the tsar's wife she would weave linen for the entire kingdom. The third sister said that she would give the tsar an heir "handsome and fearless without compare." She wanted to give birth to a great warrior, and employ the other two sisters in her charge. Tsar Saltan decided to marry this sister that very night, making the other two sisters very envious.

Tsar Saltan soon went away to war. During his absence, his queen gave birth to a healthy baby boy named Gvidon. Her jealous sisters changed the note which she wrote to her husband. In this note the sisters wrote that the queen gave birth to neither a boy nor a girl, but to a creature. When the tsar read the note, he was very upset and wrote back for the queen not to take any action, but rather wait for his return. The evil sisters changed the note, and wrote that the tsar wished for his wife and son to be put into a barrel and thrown into the sea. The palace guards couldn't disobey the tsar's orders, so they put the queen and her son inside the barrel and rolled it into the water.

The barrel drifted for many years, finally washing ashore. By this time, prince Gvidon was a grown man. At this shore, the prince rescued a swan being attacked by an evil magician who was in the form of a black hawk. The swan then turned into a beautiful princess. The prince then became ruler of that land, and his kingdom became famous throughout the world.

The rumors about this great kingdom reached Tsar Saltan as told by a merchant. And the tsar made plans to travel there, but

the evil sisters talked him out of it. The next time the merchant passed through the kingdom of Prince Gvidon he saw the Magic Squirrel, which lived in a crystal cage that Prince Gvidon had built for it. Again the merchant arrived home to tell Tsar Saltan of his son's magical land, but again the evil sisters interfered. They told the tsar that he should instead go to the land where one can see thity-three warriors and Chernomor rise from the ocean.

The Princess Swan explained to Prince Gvidon that these warriors were her brothers, so when the merchant passed through the land a third time, this feat was performed for him. Having heard this story, the wicked sisters dissuaded the Tsar once more from traveling to his son by telling him that it would be more worth his while to find the Magic Princess with the Sea Star above her head.

Prince Gvidon was sad when he discovered once more that his father would not come to see him. Little did he know that the Swan Princess and the Magic Princess were one in the same! The merchant then returned home a fourth time to inform the tsar that his son had married the Magic Princess. The tsar then immediately set sail for Gvidon's kingdom where the family was reunited. When he reached the island, Prince Gvidon was there to meet the tsar. Gvidon led him, along with his two sisters-in-law to the palace. Along the way, the tsar saw everything that he had heard so much about. There at the gates were the thirty-three knights and old Chernomor, standing guard. In the courtyard was the Magic Squirrel, singing a song and gnawing on a golden nut. In the garden was the beautiful princess, Gvidon's wife. And then the tsar saw something unexpected: there standing next to the princess was Gvidon's mother, the tsar's long-lost wife. The tsar recognized her immediately. With tears streaming down his cheeks, he rushed to embrace her, and years of heartache were now forgotten. He then realized that Prince Gvidon was his son, and the two threw their arms around each other as well.

A merry feast was held. The two sisters hid in shame. The tsar, queen, prince Gvidon and the princess lived the rest of their days in happiness.

Baklazhanovaya Ikra

Eggplant Caviar

Serves 6

Ingredients:
1 large eggplant
1 onion
2 tomatoes
2 garlic cloves
2 tablespoons vinegar
2 tablespoons vegetable oil
Salt and pepper to taste
Fresh parsley

Method:
Pierce an eggplant with a fork in several places. Put on a baking sheet and bake at 450 degrees F, turning while baking, for an hour or until soft. Cool down. Cut the eggplant lengthwise into two halves. Scoop out the pulp and chop until very fine. Chop onion very finely, peel tomatoes and chop, mince garlic cloves. Mix onion, tomatoes and pulp, garlic, oil, vinegar. Stir thoroughly and season with salt and pepper. Cover and refrigerate for several hours. Baklazhanovaya Ikra is served with chopped parsley.

Serving suggestion: Garnish with chopped parsley or cilantro.

Tale of the Fox and the Hare

This fable, with a moral to the story, is a very popular type of tale amongst Russian folklore.

Once upon a time, deep in the forest, there lived a Fox and a Hare. The Fox's house was very large and spacious, but it was made of ice and always melted in the spring. The Hare's house was made of birch bark, but it was tiny.

Spring came and the Fox knew that she had to move to a new house, but she didn't want to build one. The Fox decided to trick the Hare into coming out so that the she could get in. The Fox knocked on the door and told the Hare that she needed water to put out a fire. Once the Hare came out the Fox jumped in and locked the door.

The Hare knocked at the door and cried helplessly for the Fox to get out, but to no avail. The sneaky Fox didn't respond. Poor Hare didn't sleep that night because it was very cold in the forest. In the morning he decided to go to the Wolf. "Dear Wolf! Please help me! The Fox has stolen my home!" "Don't worry! I will kick the Fox out of your house," the Wolf calmed the Hare.

When they came to the Hare's home, the Wolf knocked at the door and said, "Fox, open the door! You have stolen the Hare's home! Come out!"

The Fox answered, "Who is knocking at the door? If you are the Wolf you may come in. I will kill you at once." The Wolf was frightened to death and rushed to the forest never to be heard from again.

The Hare was very upset and decided to call the Bear for help. The Bear agreed to help the Hare. The Fox found out that the Bear had agreed to help the Hare to kick her out of the house. She went to the forest, took down a hornet's nest from a tree and put it on the home's porch. The Bear came to the house and roared, "Fox, come out of the house! Otherwise I will ruin the house and kill you!" At that moment, the Bear stepped on the hornet's nest and screamed from pain. Hornets stung the Bear's foot and then his neck, ears, and even his tail. The Bear ran away wailing.

The Hare was very sad. He was walking through the forest and met a brave Cockerel. "'Why are you crying little Hare?" asked the Cockerel.

"The Fox has stolen my house from me! Now I am homeless! I will have to spend the night in the cold and dark forest," said the Hare bitterly. "Don't be afraid! I will help you," answered the Cockerel. The Cockerel noticed a big pipe lying in the grass nearby. The Cockerel took it and put it on two big logs, which came to resemble a field gun. Then the Cockerel began to shout loudly, "Listen to my command, soldiers! Fire your weapons at this house!" The Fox looked out of the window and saw the big field gun and a soldier. This time the Fox was very frightened. She believed that the army came and soldiers were going to fire at the house. So, the Fox ran away and was never seen again. The Cockerel and the Hare became friends and lived in the house together.

Beet Salad

Serves 6

Ingredients:
2 beets
2 pickled cucumbers
2 garlic cloves
5 dried prunes
1/2 cup of chopped walnuts
2 tablespoons mayonnaise

Method:
Boil and peel the beets. Grate beets and pickles; chop garlic cloves, walnuts and prunes finely. Combine all ingredients and stir in mayonnaise.

Tale of the Scarlet Flower

Once upon a time in a land far away, a merchant had three daughters, whom he loved very much. As the merchant was preparing to set out on a long journey, he asked all of them what they would like for him to bring back from the exotic lands. The first daughter asked for a golden crown, and the second one requested a crystal mirror. The third daughter simply asked for a little scarlet flower.

The merchant set out on his journey. It was not long before he found a beautiful golden crown and a crystal mirror. He had great difficulty finding the third gift, the scarlet flower. He searched everywhere, and finally his search led him into an enchanted forest. The merchant stumbled across a big palace, deep within these woods. He went closer and saw a courtyard. Once he entered the courtyard, he noticed that there grew a beautiful flower. As the merchant drew closer to the flower, he realized what it was--the scarlet flower, which his youngest daughter wanted so much. As soon as he picked the scarlet flower, a hideous beast appeared. Then beast demanded that in order to spare the merchant's life, he must send one of his daughters into the enchanted forest to live with the beast forever.

The merchant returned home and gave each daughter her gift. He gave the scarlet flower to the third daughter and told her about his encounter with the beast. She agreed to go into the forest and live with the beast. She found the castle in the forest where she would dwell forever. For awhile, she lived there very happily. The beast had not revealed himself to her, and showered her daily with kindness and gifts. She started to grow quite fond of the beast, and one day asked that he show himself.

The beast finally gave in to her plea, and just as he had feared, she fainted in terror at the site of him.

That night, the girl had a dream that her father had become very ill. She begged the beast to release her so that she could go to her dying father. Saddened by her worries, the beast let her go on one condition: that she return to him in three days time. The girl went to see her sick father, and prepared to return to the beast within the three days time. However, her sisters changed the time on the clocks, making her arrive late. Upon her arrival, the girl was horrified to find the beast dead, lying there holding her scarlet flower. Sobbing, the girl embraced the dead beast and professed her love for him. Her love for him broke an ancient spell which was once cast on him by an evil witch. And the beast awoke, turning into a handsome prince.

They were married at once and lived happily ever after.

Givech

Sauteed Vegetables

Serves 8

Description: This is one of my personal favorites—an eggplant lover's delight. This dish can be served as an appetizer, or with the main course.

Ingredients:
2 eggplant
3 red bell peppers
3 tomatoes
3 carrots
1 onion
2 zucchini
Salt to taste
Pepper to taste
Paprika to taste

Method:
Chop up eggplant, red bell peppers, tomatoes, carrots, onions, and zucchini into 1/2 inch cubes. In a large size skillet, sauté onions until golden brown. Add the eggplant, red bell peppers, tomatoes, carrots and zucchini. Add salt, paprika and pepper. Stir on low flame and cover. Cook for 1/2 an hour.

Serving suggestion: Serve chilled and garnish with dill. Decorate with black pitted olives arranged around the platter.

Tale of Emelya and the Magic Pike

Once upon a time there lived an old man who had three sons, two of them clever young men and the third, Emelya, a fool. The two elder brothers were always at work, while Emelya lay on the stove ledge all day long without a care in the world. One day when the older brothers set out to work, they ordered Emelya to obey their wives.

"Emelya, obey our wives and do as they say and we will bring you nice presents from the market." After the brothers have left the house, one of the wives said, "Emelya, instead of lying on the stove all day, go and fetch some water."

Emelya took the pails and went to the water hole. He drew the water and there was a pike in one of the pails. To his surprise, the pike spoke to him in a human voice and said, "Please don't eat me. Put me back in the water and I will do anything you wish."

"What you will do for me?" asked Emelya.

"Just make a wish and it will be granted. First you have to say 'By the pike's command'," replied the fish.

Emelya ordered, "By the pike's command, I want these pails of water to go home by themselves without spilling a drop!"

As soon as Emelya said this, the pails went over the hills, all the way home without spilling a drop, and stood on their regular place. The brothers' wives saw this and were very amazed. They said, "He is not a fool. He is indeed clever - otherwise how could the pails have come home by themselves?" And they decided to give him another chore. "Don't lie on the stove. Go and fetch wood so that we can cook dinner."

Emelya sat in the sled and whispered, "By the pike's command, go into the woods, sled!" The sled took off into the woods.

In the woods Emelya commanded, "By the pike's command, axes, cut wood!" The wood was chopped and set evenly on the sled. Emelya sat on top of the wood and the sled took off back home.

The king heard rumors about Emelya and his commands being fulfilled. He sent one of the palace guards to bring Emelya to him. Emelya arrived at the palace sitting on the stove, which drove by itself. The king wanted to imprison him, but his youngest daughter suddenly fell in love with Emelya. She begged her father to let him go and to let her marry him. The king couldn't dissuade her daughter from her decision. He was very angry with his daughter, but gave his consent to their wedding. After the wedding, the king put the newlyweds into a barrel and threw it into the sea.

The barrel sailed on the water for some time. Finally, Emelya ordered, "By the pike's command, let this barrel be thrown on the shore." They climbed out of the barrel and Emelya's wife asked him to build a house for them.

Emelya commanded, "By the pike's command, let a marble palace be built opposite the king's palace!" His wish was at once fulfilled.

The next morning the king saw the beautiful palace and sent his guards to find out who was living in it. When he heard that it belonged to Emelya and his daughter, he called them to appear before him. The king blessed the newlyweds from the bottom of his heart.

Emelya and his bride lived happily in their beautiful marble palace.

Cabbage Pierog

Serves 8

Ingredients:
3 cups flour
1 pound sweet butter, divided
3/4 cup cold water
2 teaspoon salt, divided
1 tablespoon rum or vodka
2 pounds cabbage
1 teaspoon sugar
3 eggs, hard-boiled, peeled, and chopped
Milk
1 egg yolk

Method:
To make the dough, combine the flour with 1/2 pound cold sweet butter (2 sticks), cutting it up. Mix together the water, 1 teaspoon salt, and the rum or vodka. Add this to the flour mixture and mix. Roll out the dough into a rectangle about 1/2 inch thick. Fold into thirds, seal in a plastic bag, and refrigerate for a few hours.

Bring one stick butter (1/4 pound) to room temperature. Roll out dough again to a thickness of 1/2 inch and spread butter on it. Fold into thirds and roll again. Fold the dough again, and place in airtight plastic in refrigerator. Finely shred the cabbage. Put cabbage in a pan with enough milk to cover 1/2 the depth of the cabbage. Add 1 teaspoon sugar and 1 teaspoon salt. Mix and cook, uncovered, until cabbage is soft. Drain well. In the pan that you used to cook the cabbage, melt the remaining stick of butter. Add the cabbage and the chopped hard-boiled eggs.

Preheat oven to 450 degrees F. Butter a 9x12 inch pan. Take 3/4 of the dough, roll it into a rectangle slightly larger than the pan, bringing the dough up the sides and cutting off the excess. Spread cabbage mixture over top. Roll out remaining dough and place over top. Pinch edges to seal. Brush with an egg wash that you have made by combining the egg yolk and 1 teaspoon water. Make holes in the top of the pie to let steam escape during cooking. Bake for approximately 45 minutes.

Tale of the Snowmaiden

Once upon a time, a peasant woman looked out the window of her cottage to watch the village children play in the snow. She did this often because the woman and her husband had no children of their own, and their biggest wish was to one day be able to watch their own child play in the snow.

The husband one day suggested to his wife that they should go outside and build a snowman instead of sitting in the house all day. The wife agreed, but wanted instead to build a girl—a snowmaiden. The couple went out into the garden and began to build a snowmaiden. They used two deep blue beads for eyes, made two dimples in her cheeks, and a piece of red ribbon for her mouth. All of a sudden, Snowmaiden's mouth began to smile; her hair began to curl. She began to move her arms and legs and then she walked through the garden and into the cottage. The couple couldn't believe their eyes. Now they had their own daughter and what a joy it was!

Snowmaiden grew, not by the day, but by the hour. And with each day she grew more beautiful. The proud couple wouldn't let her out of their sight. They doted on her. Snowmaiden was as white as the snow, her eyes were like deep blue beads, and her blond hair reached down to her waist. But she didn't have any color in her cheeks or lips. Still, she was so beautiful!

As winter melted into spring, and the weather started getting warmer, Snowmaiden started to behave strangely. She no longer wanted to go outside to play with the other children, and she began to hide in the dark places of the house. The husband and wife began to worry about her.

Soon summer came and Snowmaiden was more withdrawn than ever. One day, her friends asked her to join them on a trip

into the woods to pick berries. Snowmaiden was reluctant to join, but at the persistence of her parents, went along. Snowmaiden took a little basket and went into the forest with her friends. Her friends walked about the forest, wove garlands of flowers, and sang songs. But Snowmaiden found a cool stream and sat by it. She sat looking at it and dipped her fingers in it, playing with the droplets. Evening came. The girls played even more merrily; wearing their garlands, they built a bonfire and began jumping over it. Snowmaiden was reluctant to play with them. But as the night went on, Snowmaiden grew very lonely by herself, and decided to join their games. "Jump over the fire!" her friends yelled at her. Snowmaiden took a step, ran towards the fire, jumped, and melted away.

Rediska So Smetanoi

Radishes with Sour Cream

This makes a great summer salad.

Serves 4

Ingredients:
20 small, round radishes
1 egg, hard-boiled
1/4 cup of sour cream

Method:
Thinly slice the hard-boiled egg and chop into cubes. Thinly slice the radishes into circles. Combine the chopped egg, radishes, and sour cream and mix well.

Serving suggestion: Arrange the mixture on a glass plate and garnish with dill.

Tale of Geese and Swans

Once upon a time, in a small cottage lived a man and his wife. They had a daughter and a little son who brought them lots of joy. One day the mother said to her daughter, "Darling daughter, your father and I will go to work so that we can earn money. Take care of your brother, and don't leave him alone. Be a good girl and we will buy you presents."

Once the parents left the house, the girl forgot all about her parents' instructions, and left her little brother in the garden next to the house. She ran outside to play with her friends.

While the girl was absorbed in playing games with her friends, Magical Geese and Swans flew down and stole her little brother out of the garden. The girl returned home, only to discover that her brother was gone. She cried, calling for her little brother. While she was weeping, in the field she saw the birds in the sky. She suddenly remembered that people always said that Geese and Swans frequently stole little children. She started running after the birds. She ran fast trying to catch up with them.

She ran after them into a field when she saw a Stove. The girl asked the Stove it if it had seen the Geese and Swans. The Stove answered, "If you eat my rye patty, I will tell you."

The girl replied, "I won't eat your rye patties. I don't even eat them at home." The Stove did not show her the direction.

The girl kept on running when she stumbled upon an Apple Tree and asked it if it had seen the Geese and Swans.

The Apple Tree answered, "Eat my wild apple and I will tell you."

The girl responded, "I won't eat your wild apple. I don't eat even eat apples from my garden at home." The Apple Tree

didn't show her the direction.

She ran farther and farther, and she saw a River of Milk with Shores of Pudding. The girl asked, "Milk River, Shores of Pudding, could you tell me in what direction Geese and Swans have flown carrying my little brother?"

The Milk River replied, "If you eat my pudding with milk I will show you the direction."

"I don't eat even cream at home," the girl answered.

The girl kept running through the forest and fields, frantically trying to find her little brother. It was getting dark when she saw a little hut that stood on chicken legs and turned itself around. She went inside and saw her little brother sitting on the bench and playing with silver apples. In the hut was old Baba Yaga the Witch, spinning yarn. The girl quickly grabbed her brother and started to run away. Baba Yaga ordered the Geese and Swans to fly after them. Frightened, the girl started looking for a place to hide.

The girl and her little brother reached the Milk River and noticed that Geese and Swans were in closing in.

"Dear Milk River, please hide us," the girl begged.

"Eat my pudding with milk."

The children ate pudding and milk. The Milk River hid them beneath its shore. The Geese and Swans didn't see them and flew by. The children continued to run but soon they noticed that the Geese and Swans were catching up.

They saw the Apple Tree and the girl begged, "Dear Apple Tree, please hide us!"

"Eat my wild apples."

The children ate the apples. The Apple Tree covered them with its branches and leaves. Once again, the Geese and Swans didn't notice them and flew by. The girl and her brother continued running. The birds saw them. They now came very close; they began to strike at them with their wings. Luckily she saw the Stove in her path.

"Dear Stove, please hide us!" she begged.

"Eat my cake of rye" replied the Stove.

The children ate the rye cake and hid themselves in the Stove.

The Geese and Swans could not find the sister and brother, and they flew away. The children thanked the Stove and went home.

Luckily, as soon as the children returned home, their parents came home from work. To this day the children promised not to worry their parents again.

Pashtet

Liver Pate

Serves 8

Ingredients:
1 pound chicken livers or calves liver
1 tablespoon salt
2 large onions
1/3 cup butter
Pepper to taste
1 large egg
2 slices of white bread, crusts removed
1/2 cup chicken stock
1/2 garlic clove, minced

Method:
Cut the liver into strips. Chop up the onions. In a large skillet, melt the butter; add the onions and garlic. Fry until they begin to brown, then add the liver and continue to fry for 8 to 12 minutes until the livers are no longer showing any pink. Put the ingredients into blender or food processor and chop until the mixture is smooth and well blended. Grease a casserole dish and turn out the liver mixture into it. Preheat the oven to 350 degrees F. Bake the mixture for 45 minutes. Remove and let cool down. Refrigerate for 30 minutes prior to serving.

Serving suggestion: Serve in a bowl accompanied by toast or crackers.

Tale of the Humpbacked Little Pony

Once upon a time, in a land far away, a peasant had three sons. Of the three, Ivan was not the brightest and was considered to be the village fool. One day Ivan went into town and bought three horses. Two of the horses were beautiful stallions—fast and strong. The third horse had a limp and was hunchbacked. Ivan brought them home and put them in the stable. The next day Ivan went outside to care for his new horses, but when he opened the stable doors he found that his two stallions had been abducted. The Little Humpbacked Pony was not taken.

Before long, the little horse began to display unusual magical powers. He could alter his appearance and fly. Ivan grew to love his Little Humpbacked Pony greatly. The word got around the entire kingdom and people flocked to see this magical horse.

The news of the Little Humpbacked Pony reached the tsar. The tsar ordered Ivan to bring the horse to him at once. Once the tsar saw what incredible powers the horse possessed, he ordered Ivan to have the horse stay and work in his palace. The tsar became very greedy and demanding of the Little Humpbacked Pony. He ordered the pony to catch the elusive Fire Bird, and used it to fly to the Moon Palace. Then the tsar requested that the magic horse find the beautiful Maiden Queen and bring her to him to become his wife.

The Little Humpbacked Pony fulfilled the tsar's commands and found the beautiful Maiden Queen. The queen was not at all pleased with the mean and old tsar's company. She was

actually very fond of Ivan, who had already fallen in love with her. The Maiden Queen was very shrewd, and she came up with a plan to get rid of the greedy old man. She demanded that the tsar would have to perform a special ritual to turn himself into a good-looking, young man. He would have to first jump into a bath full of cold water, then into one of boiling water, and lastly into one of boiling milk. The tsar, being cowardly, ordered Ivan to test the bath ritual. So Ivan sat in each bath, being protected by his magical pony. He emerged from the third a handsome young man. Having witnessed this transformation the tsar quickly undressed and jumped into the cold water. Then he jumped into the second bath tub in which he was boiled, and never emerged.

Soon after the tsar's death, Ivan and the Maiden Queen were married, and they lived happily ever after with their Little Humpbacked Pony.

Stolichnyi Salat

Capital Salad

A light, refreshing blend of fruits and vegetables, this salad is named after the capital of Russia.

Serves 8

Ingredients:
2 scallions, chopped
1 red apple, cored
1 green apple, cored
4 red skin potatoes
1/2 pound chicken meat, cooked and cut into 1/2 inch cubes
1 large carrot, peeled
3/4 cup green peas
1 orange, peeled
3 egg yolks, hard-boiled
3 tablespoons olive oil
3/4 cup mayonnaise
3/4 cup sour cream or plain yogurt
2 tablespoons cider vinegar
1/2 teaspoons salt
Ground pepper to taste
1 tablespoons white wine vinegar
1/4 cup parsley fresh chopped
1/4 cup dill fresh chopped

Method:
Chop apples, leaving the skin on. Boil the potatoes in salted water, then drain, peel, and cut them into cubes 1/2 inch in size.

Boil the carrot until just tender. Remove and cut into rounds 1/4 inch in thickness. Boil peas in the salted water from the potatoes for 5 minutes and drain. Section the orange, remove the section membranes, and cut into 1 inch chunks. Mix the fruit and vegetables together with the cooked chicken cubes. Press the egg yolks with a fork and mix with 2 teaspoons of olive oil until a smooth, creamy paste is formed. Stir in 2 teaspoons of the cider vinegar and 1/2 cup of the mayonnaise and the sour cream or yogurt. Add pepper and salt. Pour the dressing over the warm vegetables, toss, and cover. Refrigerate for 6 hours. Mix the remaining ingredients together. Pour the ingredients over the salad and sprinkle with dill and parsley.

Serving suggestion: Serve on a bed of red cabbage leaves.

Tale of Masha and the Bear

Once upon a time, long ago, there lived a grandfather and grandmother, and with them their little granddaughter Masha. One day Masha asked to go into the forest to gather mushrooms. "Go my little granddaughter, but please don't get lost!" they said. Masha wandered about the forest and got lost. Suddenly she saw a small wooden hut. The girl went inside the hut, but no one was there. "Who lives here? Where is the owner?" she called. Little did she know that in there lived a big Bear. In the evening the Bear returned home, saw Masha, and was very happy!

"You will live with me now. You will stoke my stove. You will make my porridge. You will feed me porridge—you will take care of me forever!" the Bear announced. Masha began living in the Bear's hut.

Every morning the Bear went to gather food in the forest. He instructed Masha not to leave the hut and if she tried to escape, he threatened to catch her and eat her. Masha began to think of ways she could get away from the Bear. The deep and dark forest was all around, and she didn't know her way home.

At last Masha came up with a plan. She baked some pies and put them in a great big basket. "Bear, please let me have a day off so I can go into the village and take these pies to Grandmother and Grandfather," she said.

"No, I will take the pies myself," said the Bear.

"On the way, don't open the basket, and don't eat the pies. I will be watching you from a tall tree in the forest all day long," warned Masha.

"I will do as you say." answered the Bear. Masha placed the pies in the basket. To distract the Bear, Masha told him to go outside and check the weather. As soon as the Bear went outside, Masha climbed into the basket. She put the big plate with the pies on her head. The Bear came back in, picked up the basket, and was on his way to the village.

The Bear walked through the forest and got tired. "I will sit on this stump and eat the pies." he said.

"I see you! I see you! Don't sit on the stump and don't eat the pies! Take them to Grandmother and Grandfather!" shouted Masha.

The Bear looked up at the trees and thought that she must be sitting very high up in the tree to see everything. The Bear came to the village. He knocked on the grandparents door and shouted, "Open up quickly! I have brought pies to you from Masha!" The dog saw the Bear and ran straight at him! The Bear got so scared that he dropped the basket, and ran back into the forest. Grandfather and Grandmother came out, opened the basket, and there was Masha! Grandfather and Grandmother were so very happy, they began hugging and kissing Masha. They brought her into the house and fed her a warm apple pie.

Syelodka Pod Shuboi

Herring in a Fur Coat

Herring is an important part of Russian cuisine. This mouth-watering dish is layered into a perfect blend of herring and vegetables.

Serves 6

Ingredients:
3/4 pound salt herring
2 boiled potatoes
2 large boiled beets
6 medium scallions
1 cup mayonnaise
Parsley sprigs

Method:
Chop the herring crosswise into 1 inch pieces. Peel the potatoes and beets, and dice them into 1/2 inch pieces. Chop scallions into 1/4 inch pieces. Spread all of the herring pieces on the bottom of the serving bowl. Layer the scallions on top of the herring, followed by a layer of the potatoes, and then a layer of beets. For the final layer, spread the mayonnaise over the beets. The salad should be covered with plastic wrap and refrigerated for up to 5 hours.

Serving suggestions: Decorate with parsley sprigs and olives. Serve chilled.

Tale of Leafy Tops and the Roots

Once upon a time, a peasant wanted to plant a turnip in the forest. He went to the forest, plowed the land and was about to sow seeds. Suddenly, a big Bear approached the peasant and said, "How dare you sow a turnip seed in my forest? I will eat you now!"

The peasant begged the Bear for mercy and promised to share the harvest with him. "You will take the leafy tops of the turnips and I will take the roots," said the peasant. The Bear agreed not to eat him in return for the leafy tops.

Once autumn came, the peasant came to the forest to harvest the turnips. He kept his promise and gave the Bear the leafy tops of the turnips. The peasant loaded the harvest on the wagon and headed off to the market to sell the turnips. The Bear asked the peasant to let him taste the roots.

The Bear tasted the roots of the turnip and growled, "You tricked me! Your roots are tasty! Next time I will take roots and you will take the leafy tops." The peasant agreed.

The year after, he planted rye. The Bear was already waiting for him in the forest. The peasant gave the Bear roots and went to a mill to thresh the grain. The Bear started chewing the roots. They were tasteless. The Bear realized that the peasant had deceived him again and angrily told him to never plant anything in the forest.

Ever since that time, it came to be that the peasants sow seeds in the field, and the Bears gather mushrooms and pick berries in the forest.

Garlic Cheese

Serves 10

Ingredients:
1 pound Danish Havarti cheese
2 tablespoons mayonnaise
2 gloves garlic, crushed

Method:
Mince the cheese by processing it briefly in a food processor. The cheese should be grainy. Add the remaining ingredients, mix well, and refrigerate.

Serving suggestion: Serve in a decorative bowl, accompanied by crackers or chips.

Soups

Soups are an important part of a Russian meal, usually served after the appetizers. A meal is not considered complete without one of these recipes.

Borscht

Beet Soup

This popular beet soup tastes great when served steaming-hot during the cold winter. It can also be served cold on hot summer days.

Serves 8

Ingredients:
2 tablespoons of butter
1/2 cup onion, finely chopped
3 beets, peeled and cut into strips 1/8 inch wide by 2 inches long
1 teaspoon sugar
1 small can tomato paste
2 tomatoes, peeled, seeded, and coarsely chopped
2 teaspoons of salt
Freshly ground black pepper
2 quarts of beef stock
1/2 pound of white cabbage, quartered, cored, and shredded
1 pound boiled beef brisket cut into 1 inch cubes
1 bay leaf
1/2 cup fresh dill or parsley, finely chopped

Method:
In a 6 to 8-quart pot, melt the butter. Add the onions, stirring frequently until they are soft but not brown. Stir in the beets, then add the tomato paste, sugar, chopped tomatoes, 1 teaspoon of salt and a few grindings of black pepper. Pour in 1/2 cup of stock, cover the pot, and simmer for 50 minutes.

Pour the remaining stock into the pot and add the chopped

cabbage. Bring to a boil, and then add the beef. Stir parsley and bay leaf into the soup, and add another teaspoon of salt. Simmer, partially covered, for 1/ 2 hour.

Serving suggestion: Place a bowl of sour cream at the table. Each diner can add a teaspoon to the borscht.

Tale of Morozko

Father Frost

In Russia, Morozko has always been an important figure to all kids during the winter season. He is like Santa Clause, bringing presents during holidays. It is customary for the parents to place the gifts under the Christmas tree, letting the kids believe that it was Father Frost. This is a popular fable about him rewarding the good deeds and punishing the bad ones.

Once upon a time, long ago, there lived an old widower and his daughter. The widower decided that it was time for him to remarry. He found a wife who had a daughter herself from a previous marriage. The woman spoiled her own daughter, praising her at every opportunity, but she despised her stepdaughter.

The new wife found fault with everything the stepdaughter did, and made her work hard—day and night. One day, in the middle of a terrible winter, the wife decided that she could get rid of the girl by having her husband take her deep into the woods and leave her there to freeze. The stepmother ordered the husband to carry out this wish. He, of course, did not want to agree to this, but he was also afraid of the woman. So he wept as he reluctantly took his daughter into the forest and left her.

The girl sat in the snow, freezing and alone, under a tree. All of a sudden she heard the breaking and snapping of branches, and then a voice spoke. "Are you warm my child?" it said. The voice belonged to Morozko.

She replied, "Yes Father Frost, I'm quite warm," even though she was freezing cold.

At first, Morozko had wanted to freeze the life out of her with his icy grip. But he admired the young girl's bravery and felt sorry for her. He gave her a warm fur coat and downy quilts before he left. Later in the night, Morozko returned to check on the girl. This time Morozko brought a large box for her to sit on. A little later, Morozko returned once more to ask how she was doing. She was doing quite well now, and this time Morozko gave her silver and gold jewelry to wear—with enough extra jewels to fill the box upon which she was sitting!

The next day the husband returned to take his daughter's body. He was overjoyed to find her alive and dressed warmly, covered with riches. Upon their return home, the jealous wife then insisted that her own daughter be left in the forest overnight, hoping that she too would return wealthy.

Again the husband drove deep into the woods, this time leaving his stepdaughter there. As the night wore on she also heard the voice of Father Frost. "Are you warm my child?" he asked.

The girl, being spoiled and rude, replied, "Of course not, are you blind? Can't you see? Now leave me alone!" Father Frost was enraged with her reply and sent the coldest frost that there had ever been.

When the husband drove into the woods the next day, he didn't return with a girl adorned in riches as his wife expected, but with her cold frozen body instead. Once he returned home he took his daughter and left his evil wife.

The husband and his daughter lived happily ever after.

Rassolnick

Tart Sorrel Soup

Serves 6

Ingredients:
1 large dill pickle
6 tablespoons of butter
1 cup onion, thinly sliced
1/2 cup celery, finely chopped
1 cup parsley, finely chopped
2 pounds fresh sorrel leaves, stripped from their stems and coarsely chopped
1/4 pound fresh spinach leaves, stripped from their stems and coarsely chopped
2 teaspoon of salt
Freshly ground black pepper to taste
2 quarts of beef stock
1/2 pound of veal
1/2 cup of flour
2 tablespoons of vegetable oil
1 egg yolk

Method:
Cut the pickle in half lengthwise and run a small spoon down its length to remove the seeds and pulp. Place the seeds and pulp in a fine sieve set over a small bowl and press them firmly with the back of a spoon to extract all their juices. Discard the seeds and pulp and set the juice aside. Chop the pickle as finely a possible.

Melt 4 tablespoons of the butter in a 3 to 4-quart casserole over medium heat. Stir in the onions and celery, and cover the pan. Reduce the heat to low and simmer gently until the onions are soft. Add the pickle, parsley, sorrel, and spinach. Stir in the salt and a few grindings of pepper. Pour in the beef stock, stir, and bring to a boil over high heat. Then reduce the heat to low, partially cover the pan, and simmer for about 20 minutes.

Slice the veal into 1 inch cubes. Dip the slices in the flour one at a time. Heat the remaining 2 tablespoons of butter and the 2 tablespoons of oil in a skillet set over high heat. Place the floured slices of veal into the skillet, and cook until they are browned. Transfer the veal to the simmering soup. Bring the soup to a boil and stir in the pickle juice.

In a mixing bowl, beat the egg yolk lightly with a fork. Slowly beat in 1 cup of the hot soup, and then pour the egg mixture slowly into the casserole, stirring constantly. Simmer a moment or two without letting it come to a boil.

Tale of the Wise Girl

Once upon a time, there was a little village where nearly all the inhabitants bred horses. It was the month of October, when a big livestock market was held yearly in the main town nearby. Two brothers, one rich and the other one poor, set off for market. The rich man rode a stallion, and the poor brother a young mare.

At dusk, they stopped beside an empty hut and tethered their horses outside before going to sleep themselves on two heaps of straw. Great was their surprise when next morning they saw three horses outside, instead of two. Well, to be exact, the newcomer was not really a horse. It was a foal, to which the mare had given birth during the night. Soon it had the strength to struggle to its feet, and after a drink of its mother's milk, the foal staggered its first few steps. The stallion greeted it with a cheerful whinny, and when the two brothers set eyes on it for the first time, the foal was standing beside the stallion.

"It belongs to me!" exclaimed Dimitri, the rich brother, the minute he saw it. "It's my stallion's foal." Ivan, the poor brother, began to laugh.

"Whoever heard of a stallion having a foal? It was born to my mare!"

"No, that's not true! It was standing close to the stallion, so it's the stallion's foal. And therefore it's mine!"

The brothers started to quarrel, and they decided to go to town and bring the matter before the judges. Still arguing, they headed for the big square where the courtroom stood. But what they didn't know was that it was a special day—the day when, once a year, the Emperor himself administered the law. He himself received all who came seeking justice. The brothers were ushered into his presence, and they told him all about the dispute.

Of course, the Emperor knew perfectly well who the owner of the foal was. He was on the point of proclaiming in favor of the poor brother, when suddenly Ivan developed an unfortunate twitch in his eye. The Emperor was greatly annoyed by this familiarity by a humble peasant, and decided to punish Ivan for his disrespect. After listening to both sides of the story, he declared it was difficult— indeed impossible—to say exactly who was the foal's rightful owner.

Being in the mood for a spot of fun (he loved posing riddles and solving them as well), to the amusement of his counselors the Emperor exclaimed, "I can't judge which of you should have the foal, so it will be awarded to whichever of you solves the following four riddles: what is the fastest thing in the world? What is the fattest? What's the softest, and what is the most precious? I command you to return to the palace in a week's time with your answers!"

Dimitri started to puzzle over the answers as soon as he left the courtroom. When he reached home though, he realized he had nobody to help him.

"Well, I will just have to seek help, for if I can't solve these riddles, I will lose the foal!" Then he remembered a woman, one of his neighbors, to whom he had once lent a silver ducat. That had been some time ago, and with the interest the neighbor now owed him three ducats. And since she had a reputation for being quick-witted and very astute, he decided to ask her advice in exchange for canceling part of her debt. But the woman was not slow to show how clever she really was, and promptly demanded that the whole debt be wiped out in exchange for the answers.

"The fastest thing in the world is my husband's bay horse,"

she said. "Nothing can beat it! The fattest is our pig! Such a huge beast has never been seen! The softest is the quilt I made for the bed, using my own goose's feathers. It's the envy of all my friends. The most precious thing in the world is my three-month old nephew. There isn't a more handsome child. I wouldn't exchange him for all the gold on earth, and that makes him the most precious thing on earth!"

Dimitri was rather doubtful about the woman's answers being correct. On the other hand, he had to take some kind of solution back to the Emperor. And he guessed, quite rightly, that if he didn't, he would be punished.

In the meantime, Ivan, who was a widower, had gone back to the humble cottage where he lived with his small daughter. Only seven years old, the little girl was often left alone, and as a result was thoughtful and very clever for her age. The poor man too k the little girl into his confidence, for like his brother, he knew he would never be able to find the answers.

The child sat in silence for a moment, and then firmly said, "Tell the Emperor that the fastest thing in the world is the cold north wind in winter. The fattest is the soil in our fields whose crops give life to men and animals alike, the softest thing is a child's caress and the most precious is honesty."

The day came when the two brothers were to return before the Emperor, and they were led into his presence. The Emperor was curious to hear what they had to say, but he roared with laughter at Dimitri's foolish answers. When it was Ivan's turn to speak, a frown spread over the Emperor's face. The poor brother's wise replies made him squirm, especially the last one about honesty—the most precious thing of all.

The Emperor knew perfectly well that he had been dishonest in his dealings with the poor brother, for he had denied him justice. But he could not bear to admit it in front of his own counselors, so he angrily demanded, "Who gave you these answers?" Ivan told the Emperor that it was his small daughter.

Still annoyed, the great man said, "You shall be rewarded for having such a wise and clever daughter. You shall be awarded the foal that your brother claimed, together with a hundred silver ducats. But... But..." and the Emperor winked at his counselors, "You will come before me in seven days' time, bringing your daughter. And since she's so clever, she must appear before me neither naked nor dressed, neither on foot nor on horseback, neither bearing gifts nor empty-handed. And if she does this, you will have your reward. If not, you'll have your head chopped off for your impudence!"

The onlookers began to laugh, knowing that the poor man would never to able to fulfill the Emperor's conditions.

Ivan went home in despair, his eyes brimming with tears. But when he had told his daughter what had happened, she calmly said, "Tomorrow, go and catch a hare and a partridge. Both must be alive! You'll have the foal and the hundred silver ducats! Leave it to me!" Ivan did as his daughter said. He had no idea what the two creatures were for, but he trusted in his daughter's wisdom.

On the day of the audience with the Emperor, the palace was thronged with bystanders waiting for Ivan and his small daughter to arrive. At last, the little girl appeared—draped in fishing net, riding the hare, and holding the partridge in her hand. She was neither naked nor dressed, on foot nor on horseback.

Scowling, the Emperor told her, "I said neither bearing gifts nor empty-handed!"

At these words, the little girl held out the partridge. The Emperor stretched out his hand to grasp it, but the bird fluttered into the air. The third condition had been fulfilled. In spite of himself, the Emperor could not help admiring the little girl who had so cleverly passed such a test.

In a gentler voice, he said, "Is your father terribly poor, and does he desperately need the foal?"

"Oh, yes!" replied the little girl. "We live on the hares he catches in the rivers and the fish he picks from the trees!"

"Aha!" cried the Emperor triumphantly. "So you're not as clever as you seem to be! Who ever heard of hares in the river and fish in the trees?"

To which the little girl swiftly replied, "And who ever heard of a stallion having a foal?"

At that, both Emperor and Court burst into peals of laughter. Ivan was immediately given his hundred silver ducats and the foal, and the Emperor proclaimed, "Only in my kingdom could such a wise little girl be born!"

Meat Solianka

Meat Soup with Tomatoes, Onions, and Cucumbers

Serves 8

Ingredients:
6 cups beef stock, fresh or canned
3/4 pound beef, cut into 2 inch cubes
1/2 pound boneless shoulder of veal, trimmed of fat and cut into 1/2 inch cubes
4 tablespoons of butter
2 cups onions, thinly sliced
2 medium cucumbers, peeled, halved, seeded and cut into 1/4 inch slices
2 large tomatoes, peeled, seeded and coarsely chopped
1 teaspoon of salt
Freshly ground black pepper to taste
1 lemon, thinly sliced

Method:
In a heavy 4 to 6-quart casserole, combine the beef stock, beef and veal. Bring to a boil over high heat, skimming the top of the foam and grease as it rises to the surface. Then partially cover the casserole, reduce to medium heat, and simmer for about 1 1/2 hours or until the meat is tender enough to be easily pierced with a fork.

Meanwhile, melt 4 tablespoons of butter in a heavy 10 to 12 inch skillet over high heat. Add the onions, reduce the heat to medium, and cook 3 to 5 minutes, or until the onions are soft but not brown. Drop in the cucumbers and cook, stirring occasionally, for about 10 minutes, or until they are tender but still slightly firm. Then stir in the chopped tomatoes and cook an additional 10 minutes. Season with salt and a few grindings of black pepper, and transfer the contents of the skillet to the casserole. Add the lemon slices.

Tale of Vasilisa the Beautiful

Once upon a time, long ago in a faraway kingdom, there lived a merchant. He had a wife and a daughter—a little girl called Vasilisa the Beautiful. When Vasilisa was eight years old, her mother died. Before her death, the merchant's wife called Vasilisa to her side, took out a doll from the blanket, gave it to the girl and said, "Listen carefully and remember my words—do as I tell you. Take this doll, which has been blessed by me. Always keep the doll with you wherever you go and don't let anyone see it. If you are ever in trouble, just give the doll something to eat and ask her advice." The woman gave her daughter a last kiss and died.

After his wife's death, the merchant grieved for some time, and then decided to marry again. The merchant married a widow who had two daughters of her own. The daughters were the same age as Vasilisa. The merchant married her thinking that she would be a good housekeeper and mother, but he was wrong. His new wife turned out to be a cruel stepmother.

Vasilisa was the most beautiful girl in the kingdom. Her cruel stepmother and stepsisters were very envious of her. They made the girl do all the hard, dirty work and hoped that Vasilisa would grow thin and that her face would turn dark and ugly in the wind and sun. The girl always completed her work, and managed to grow more beautiful every day. The stepmother and her daughters gained weight and grew uglier every day. They sat around doing nothing the whole day long but gossiping and wishing bad thoughts towards Vasilisa.

Vasilisa managed to do all her difficult labor with the help of her magic doll. The girl would give her doll some delicious treat and ask it for its help and advice. After eating the treat, the doll calmed Vasilisa by telling her that everything would go well and all the work would be done. The girl just sat in the shade or picked flowers while her doll weeded the beds, watered the garden, brought pails of water from the well, lit the stove, and even gave the girl herbs against sunburn.

As the years passed and Vasilisa grew into a stunning young woman, many young men wanted her hand in marriage. No young male in the kingdom even wanted to look at her stepsisters. The stepmother began to hate Vasilisa so much that she decided get rid of the girl for once and for all.

One time the merchant went to another kingdom and wasn't expected back for some time. The stepmother decided to move to another house on the edge of the thick forest. In this forest lived the wicked witch, Baba-Yaga. This witch ate people who trespassed on her property. Every day the stepmother sent Vasilisa into the forest, hoping that Baba-Yaga would get her, but the girl always returned safe and sound with the help of her magic doll.

One cold evening the stepmother gave her daughters various tasks to do. She told Vasilisa to spin, one of her daughters to make lace, and the other one to knit stockings. She then blew out all of the candles in the house, except for a single one that burnt in the room where the girls were working, and went to bed. Some time passed and one of the stepsisters blew out the candle, pretending that she was trying to adjust the wick.

"What shall we do?" said the stepmother. "It is impossible to finish our work in the dark. Somebody should go to Baba-Yaga and ask her for a light."

"I'm not going," said the first stepdaughter who was making lace. "I can see my needle."

"I'm not going," said the second stepdaughter who was knitting stockings. "I can see my knitting needles very well."

They shoved Vasilisa out of the house to go and ask the witch for a light. The girl found herself in the dark forest. She was very scared and started to cry. Then she fed her magic doll and asked for its advice.

"Don't be afraid, Vasilisa. You will be all right. Nothing bad can happen to you while I am with you. Go to Baba-Yaga and ask her to give you a light."

Vasilisa walked through the dark forest holding the doll close and suddenly she saw a horseman riding by. His face was white, he was dressed all in white, and he was riding a white horse. After that, the first light of dawn shone across the sky.

The girl walked deeper in to the forest and saw another horseman ride by. His face was red, he was dressed in red clothes, and he was riding a red horse.

Vasilisa walked all day and at last she came to Baba-Yaga's hut. The fence around the hut was made up of human bones and crowned with human skulls. The girl was very frightened. Suddenly, she saw another horseman who galloped by. His face was black, he was dressed in black clothes, and he was riding a black horse. He rode through the gates and disappeared. After the horseman passed by, night descended and the eyes of the skulls crowning the fence began to glow. Vasilisa trembled with fear. She wanted to run away when she heard a terrible noise. The trees creaked, and the earth trembled. There was Baba-Yaga riding on her broom.

She flew up to the gate, sniffed the air and screamed, "I smell human beings! Who is here?"

Vasilisa came up to Baba-Yaga trembling with fear and said, "My name is Vasilisa. My stepmother sent me to you to ask for a light."

"I know your stepmother and her daughters. Stay here with me for a while and work. If you will work hard and complete all

66

your chores, then I will give you a light. But if you don't, I will eat you up!" The she addressed the gates, "Open up, gates! I want to come in." The gates opened, Baba-Yaga rode in, and Vasilisa walked behind her. The gates closed by themselves. They went into the hut.

Baba-Yaga stretched herself out on the bench and gave an order, "Vasilisa, bring me whatever's in the stove! I am hungry!"

The girl began to carry all of the food. There was enough of it to feed ten men. Then she went down to the cellar and brought root beer, bread, and wine. Baba-Yaga ate and drank everything. All she left Vasilisa was some cabbage soup and a crust of bread.

Before the witch went to bed, she said, "Vasilisa, you must clean the yard, sweep the hut, cook dinner, and wash the laundry. Then you must go to the corn bin and sort out the wheat, seed by seed— you have to take out all of the black bits. If you don't complete these chores I will eat you."

As soon as Baba-Yaga went to sleep, Vasilisa took her doll out of her pocket, gave her a crust of bread and said, "Little doll, please help me. Baba-Yaga has given me so many difficult tasks to do and threatened to eat me up if I do not do it."

The doll answered, "Don't be afraid, Vasilisa the Beautiful! Just eat your supper and go to bed. Mornings are wiser than evenings."

Vasilisa woke up early the next morning. She looked out the window and saw the white horseman race by, and day began to dawn. Baba-Yaga went out into the yard, whistled, and her broom appeared. The red horseman rode by, and the sun rose. Baba-Yaga climbed her broom and rode off.

Once Baba-Yaga left, Vasilisa went to the corn bin and found the doll picking out the last black bits. The other tasks were also fulfilled. The doll said, "All you have to do now is prepare dinner and after that you can have a rest."

Vasilisa thanked the doll and went to prepare dinner. In the evening the girl set the table and waited for Baba-Yaga. It grew dark. The black horseman swept by and it was night. The skulls' eyes began to shine. The trees creaked, the earth trembled, and Baba-Yaga rode in on her broom.

"Have you finished all the chores?" she asked Vasilisa.

"Yes, I have," replied the girl. Baba-Yaga was very angry; she didn't expect Vasilisa to be able to complete the chores. But there was nothing to do and she said, "Very good," and then screamed loudly, "My faithful servants! Grind the wheat!" Three pairs of hands appeared. They took the wheat and disappeared.

Baba-Yaga ate the dinner and said to Vasilisa, "Tomorrow you must do all the same things, and then you must go to the store room and sort out the dirt from the rice."

As soon as Baba-Yaga began to snore, the girl fed her doll and asked it for help. "Go to sleep. Mornings are wiser than evenings," said the doll.

The next morning Baba-Yaga rode off on her broom.

With the help of her doll, Vasilisa finished all of her chores and waited for Baba-Yaga. In the evening the witch came back, checked everything over, and sat down to eat.

"Can I ask you some questions?" said the girl.

"You may ask me, but remember that not every question has a good answer. The more one knows, the sooner one grows old."

"I just want to ask you about the men on horses I saw on the way here. First a man was riding on a white horse. His face was white and he was dressed in white. Who was he?"

"That was my Bright Day," answered Baba-Yaga.

"Then I saw a man on a red horse. He had a red face and he was dressed in red clothes. Who was he?"

"That was my Red Sun," answered Baba-Yaga.

"And then who was the black horseman who I saw while I was standing outside your gate?"

"That was my Black Night. These horsemen are my faithful servants. Now I've got a question for you. How have you managed to carry out all the work so quickly?"

"My mother's blessing helped me."

"Oh! You'd better leave then. I don't like people with blessings around here!" replied the witch.

The old woman kicked Vasilisa out of the hut, and pushed her out through the gate. Then she took one of the skulls with blazing eyes, stuck it on the end of a stick, and gave it to the girl.

"Here's light for your stepmother and her daughters. That's what you came here for, isn't it?"

Vasilisa found her way home by the light of the skull's eyes which lit up the path. She walked all night and day, and by evening she reached her home. Coming to the gates the girl was about to throw away the skull, but suddenly she heard a voice say, "You shouldn't throw me away. Your stepmother and her daughters need me."

The stepmother and stepsisters told her that there hadn't been light in the house since she had left. They tried to strike a light again and again, but to no avail. Then they tried to bring a light from the neighbors, but it always went out as they crossed the threshold.

The girl carried the skull into the house, and it fixed its eyes on the stepmother and her two daughters and burnt them like fire. They tried to hide, but couldn't get away. Vasilisa remained unharmed. She buried the skull in the garden, locked up the house, and went to live with an old woman in the nearest village.

One day she said to the old woman, "Grandmother, I would like to do something useful and help you out with money. Please go to the market and buy me the best flax you can find. I want to spin thread."

The old woman found the best thread at the market. Vasilisa spun thread that was so fine it was like hair. Then she took it and began to weave this fine thread into a beautiful cloth. The cloth was soft and rich in color and texture. The girl gave it to the old woman and said, "Grandmother, take this cloth and sell it. Keep the money for yourself because you have been so good and generous to me."

The old woman looked at it and said, "This is too precious to sell. I am going to bring this to the tsar." So she brought it to the tsar. He liked the cloth very much and asked the old woman how much she wanted for it.

The woman replied, "I can't put a price on it, Your Highness. It's a gift." The tsar thanked the old woman, loaded her with presents and she went home.

Then the tsar tried to find a tailor who could make shirts for him from this cloth. All of the tailors in the kingdom declined to work with the cloth because it was too fine for them. After his failed attempts he called the old woman and said, "You have made this cloth and you must also know how to sew shirts out of it. I would like you to make me a pair of shirts."

The old woman replied, "Your highness. It was not my work. It was made by a girl I took in."

"Take the cloth and ask this girl if she would make some shirts for me out of it."

Vasilisa made shirts from the cloth with embroidery and jewels on them. The old woman took the shirts to the tsar. Shortly after, one of the tsar's servants entered the old woman's yard. He said, "His Majesty wishes to see the girl who made his exquisite shirts. She must go to the palace to receive her reward."

Vasilisa went to the palace. As soon as the tsar saw her, he fell in love with her and asked her to be his wife. The tsar took Vasilisa by the hand and sat her down next to him. They married the next day. Vasilisa's father came back. The tsar invited him and the old woman to come and live at the palace too.

Vasilisa carried her doll around in her pocket 'til the end of her days.

Kharcho

Spicy Lamb Soup

This soup, which is popular throughout Russia, is a traditional Georgian dish.

Ingredients:
2 pounds lamb short ribs cut into 1 inch pieces
1/2 cup rice
1/2 teaspoon paprika
1/2 teaspoon fresh cilantro, chopped
1/4 teaspoon thyme
1 tablespoon parsley, chopped
3 tablespoon sunflower oil
1 quart water
2 ounces celery root
1 carrot sliced
Black pepper to taste
2 large onions, chopped
3 bay leaves
1 small can tomato paste
1/4 tablespoon hot sauce
1 teaspoon sugar
2 tablespoon lemon juice
1/4 teaspoon sage
2 teaspoons salt
3 garlic cloves, minced

Method:
In a frying pan, brown the chopped onions in oil. Add lamb pieces and garlic, and sauté for 10 minutes. Remove from heat.

Bring water to a boil in a large stockpot. Add the contents from the frying pan, 1 teaspoon of salt, and reduce heat to cook at slow boil for 30 minutes. Add all of the other ingredients and cook for 15 minutes at a slow boil. Then reduce to simmer and cook for 30 minutes.

Tale of Solovey Budimirovich

Ships frequently came to Kiev, which was the center of ancient Russia. The ships brought in foreign goods: rare precious stones, expensive cloth and furs, and gold and silver. These ships belonged to Solovey Budimirovich, who carried expensive gifts to the Prince of Kiev, Vladimir, and his wife.

Vladimir took the gifts and said, "I don't know how to pay you back. You are very rich and have more then I can offer you. Take any town you wish and rule it."

Solovey Budimirovich didn't want to take a town, but asked Vladimir to give him permission to build a crystal palace in his garden. He had fallen in love with the niece of Vladimir, whose name was Zabava. Vladimir gave his permission, and Solovey Budimirovich built the most beautiful crystal palace which was decorated with gold and precious stones.

One day, Zabava walked in the green garden and saw the amazing palace of Solovey Budimirovich. The girl began to look inside the windows. In the first window she saw Solovey's mother who was praying. In the second window she saw different riches. And in the third window she saw Solovey Budimirovich, who was singing a song.

Solovey Budimirovich noticed Zabava and invited her into the palace, where he asked her for her hand in marriage. The girl was very surprised, and accepted the marriage proposal.

Before the wedding, Solovey Budimirovich had to go to his motherland and oversee the sale of his property. Rumors started to spread across the kingdom that Solovey Budimirovich was killed on the way to his homeland.

Meanwhile, the Tatar Prince came to Kiev and demanded that Prince Vladimir give him permission to marry his niece,

Zabava. He threatened to wage war against Kiev if the prince were to deny him.

Vladimir knew that the threat was real, and there was nobody who could defend Kiev. So Vladimir reluctantly decided to give his permission to the Tatar Prince.

Shortly after Solovey Budimirovich had returned. Prince Vladimir was very glad to hear of this news because he didn't want his niece to marry the Tatar Prince.

Solovey Budimirovich and his army won the war against Tatar army and killed the Tatar Prince. Soon Solovey Budimirovich and Zabava were married and lived happily in the crystal palace surrounded by the exotic garden.

Okroshka

This meat and vegetable soup, which is served chilled, is a popular Russian dish.

Serves 6

Ingredients:
1 cup beef, cooked
1 cucumber
2 eggs, hard-boiled
3 green onions
1 teaspoon sugar
2 tablespoons Dijon mustard
1/2 cup sour cream
4 cups apple cider

Method:
Dice meat. Peel and dice cucumber and eggs. Slice green onions. Combine first 4 ingredients. Mix sugar, mustard, sour cream, and cider; beat well. Add cooked meat, and chill.

Serving suggestion: Serve sprinkled with dill.

Tale of the Wolf and the Mother Goat

Once upon a time there lived a mother goat and her kids. The goat often had to go into the forest while her children remained at home. "Lock the door, and don't let anyone in," she said. When the nanny goat came home, she knocked on the door and sang, "Dear little children, open the door, your mother has returned bringing milk."

The children heard their mother's voice and opened the door.

But a wolf also heard. When the goat left again, the wolf crept up to the little hut and sang in a gruff voice, "Dear little children; open the door, your mother has returned bringing milk."

"That is not our mother's voice! Our mother sings in a high voice!" said the baby goats. The wolf hurried to the blacksmith in the village.

"Blacksmith, Blacksmith—make me a high voice, or I will eat you up!" The Blacksmith made a high voice for the wolf. The wolf went back to the goat's little hut.

He knocked on the door and sang, "Dear little children, open the door, your mother has returned bringing milk." The little goats heard the high voice and opened the door. The wolf leapt into the hut, and grabbed all the little goats. Only the very smallest goat had climbed into the stove, and the wolf didn't find him.

The mother goat returned home. "Mama, a grey wolf came. He grabbed all of my brothers and sisters!"

"Oh no," exclaimed the mother goat. The goat went into the

forest to find the wolf.

She saw him asleep under a bush. She went toward the bush and screamed at him. The wolf jumped up and ran away, and the little goats came out safe and sound.

The goats went home, and they lived happily ever after.

Schi

Schi has taken a special place among national soups. Historians suppose that this dish was known long time ago, before the adoption of Christianity in Russia. There was a time when all soups were called Schi, but now Schi is specific to cabbage soups. These soups are cooked with meat, fish, or mushroom broths.

Serves 6

Ingredients:
1 1/2 pounds beef or chicken, bone-in
2 quarts water
1 1/2 pounds cabbage, shredded
2 large potatoes, cubed
1 turnip
1 large carrot, chopped
2 fresh tomatoes
1 onion
1 parsley root
Pepper and salt to taste
2 bay leaves

Method:
Put meat in the cold water to make broth tastier. Bring to boil; reduce heat. Remove the grease and froth from the broth surface with a spoon. Cook at a low heat for 1 hour. Pour more cold water in to keep the same quantity of broth. Add chopped carrot, shredded cabbage, and salt. Bring to boil again. Then add potatoes. Chop onion, parsley root, turnip, and tomatoes

finely and fry in a pan. Put everything in the pot and simmer at low heat for 30 minutes. Five minutes before serving, add pepper, salt, and bay leaves.

Tale of Ilya Muromets

This is a legend of Ilya, who was a fearless knight. This tale took place at a time when the Russian kingdom was under attacks by Tatars.

Ilya was the son of a peasant. He was crippled from birth and could not walk. One day, when he was a young man, several mystical men paid him a visit and said a prayer over him. They told him that it was his destiny to protect the Russian land and win victories over the Tatars.

After that, Ilya was able to walk and became unbelievably strong. His old parents were very happy that their son was healed. Iliya ordered a complete set of armor to be made, and set out to go to the city of Kiev.

On the way there, he saved the city of Chernigov from a Tatar's army. He also won a victory over the evil ruler of the Black Forest, Solovey. Ilya brought Solovey to the court of Prince Vladimir in Kiev, where he was executed.

Prince Vladimir asked that Ilya join him and lead his army of men. Ilya accepted the prince's offer and became his greatest warrior.

Ukha

Clear Salmon Soup

6 servings

Ingredients:
6 cups water
1/2 pound smelts
1 pound salmon fillet, skinned
1 large onion
1 large carrot, quartered
1 leek
1 celery stalk with leaves
1 parsnip, peeled
Salt and pepper to taste
3/4 cup white wine
3 potatoes, diced
2 thin carrots
1/2 cup scallion, chopped
Lemon slices, thin

Method:
In a large stockpot, place the water, smelts, onion, quartered
carrot, leek, celery, parsnip, and salt and pepper. Bring to a boil
over high heat, periodically skimming off the foam as it rises to
the top. Cover the pot, reduce the heat, and simmer for 40
minutes. Add the salmon, wine, potatoes, and thin carrots and
cook at a higher heat for another 40 minutes.

Serving suggestion: Ladle the stock into the bowls, sprinkle
with scallions, and garnish with lemon slices.

Tale of the Stone Flower

A long time ago in an Urals village, there lived a famous craftsman named Prokopyich. He made jewelry from malachite, and was renowned as the best gem carver in the Urals.

In the same village, there lived an orphan named Danila. He was weak and couldn't work at the factory. But he had many dreams, and liked to observe nature.

A kind old woman took Danila into her house. She taught him the lore of plants, and told him about the Stone Flower from Malachite Mountain. She told him it was the most beautiful flower in the world. But she also warned him, "Whoever finds that flower will never be happy." When Danila grew older and stronger he was sent to Prokopyich to study gem carving. Danila turned out to be extremely gifted.

One day, the owner of the factory sent him a request to make a vase from malachite. Danila began the task, but he was unsatisfied with his work. Every day he went to the woods looking for inspiration, observing flowers and plants. He worked for a long time, and at last completed a vase that he was satisfied with. When he showed it to the other craftsmen, they liked it and praised it. But Danila said, "This vase is made well, but there is no living beauty in it. When you look at the simplest flower, joy fills your heart because of its beauty. Where is there such beauty in the stone?"

One very old craftsman told him not to think that way, or he could become a servant of the Mistress of Copper Mountain. The work of humans can't compare with the work of those servants, because they have seen the Stone Flower and understand the beauty of the stone.

Danila became engaged to a very nice girl named Katya. The two were inseparable and very much in love. He wanted to carve a special vase for her.

One day Danila was in the woods looking for stone when he suddenly heard a whisper saying, "Danila, look for stone on Serpent Hill." He turned around and saw the dim outline of a woman that suddenly vanished. Right then he knew that it was the Mistress of Copper Mountain. Danila went to Serpent Hill and found a huge block of malachite. He was very happy, took the stone home, and started to carve a vase for Katya.

Soon he was disappointed with the result, and wished that he could understand the power of the stone. The day before his and Katya's wedding, he went to Serpent Hill again, sat down, and thought about how much he wanted to see that flower.

All of a sudden, the Mistress of Copper Mountain appeared before his eyes. Danila begged her to let him see the flower. She replied, "I could show it to you, but afterwards you will regret it. Those who have seen my Flower have left their families and come to live in my mountain." But Danila insisted that he had to see it. "All right," she said. "Let's go to my garden." So she took him and showed him the magical Stone Flower.

In the evening, Danila came back to the village. He couldn't stand being there. Danila was growing sadder by the minute. He broke the vase that he had been making for Katya, and ran away to Copper Mountain. No one in the village knew where he had gone. Three years passed. Katya did not marry. She was poor and didn't have any money, so she decided to try making some brooches to sell.

She went to Serpent Hill in order to find good pieces of stone. But at the hill she remembered her beloved Danila and cried. Suddenly she saw a beautiful piece of malachite. Katya took it home and carved many brooches. Katya sold her works to merchants in the village. She was always sad, though, and couldn't forget Danila. She ran again to Serpent Hill looking for another good stone. Katya realized that this was where the magic mountain was. She began to call out, "Danila, where are you?"

Then a voice answered, "He is not here!" Then suddenly the Mistress of Copper Mountain appeared and demanded, "Why did you come to my garden?"

Katya replied, "I want my Danila back. You don't have the right to take another's fiancé."

The Mistress laughed. "Do you have any idea whom you are speaking?"

Katya cried out, "I know who you are. I am not afraid of you! And I know that Danila wants to come back to me."

The Mistress said, "All right, let him speak then."

Danila appeared and the Mistress told him that he had to choose: if he went with Katya, then he would forget everything he saw and learned in the mountain. She also told him that if he decided to stay, then he would have to forget the rest of the world.

Danila answered, "I am sorry, but my heart is with Katya."

The Mistress smiled and said, "All right, Danila. Go back home. And for your honesty and loyalty, I will give you a present. You will not lose your knowledge that you have learned here. But do not tell people about the mountain. If somebody asks you where have you been, just say that you went away to improve your skill."

She then gave a box to Katya. Katya opened the box and gasped. It was filled with pebbles and jewels in vibrant colors. She picked up a plain stone of polished granite and saw the goddess blur into a spirit of grey mists and fog, with a laughter as rich as summer thunder. Then a piece of amber—and the mists swirled downward and turned into a small woman in golden robes embroidered with pine needles. A ruby, and the goddess grew tall, dressed in snapping flames. Lapis lazuli, and she turned into a cosmic mother whose robes were the night sky scattered with stars. She smiled at Katya. "Back in your world, you'll no longer see me as you just have. But the power remains coiled in each stone, responsive to a heart wise enough to understand." Then she vanished.

Katya and Danila found their way back into the world, where it was springtime. The villagers welcomed them with joy. Danila soon became famous for his wonderful stone flowers and people came from far away to admire them. Katya and Danila had children, and Danila taught them the secrets of his craft. But Katya taught them the most important thing of all—respect for the inner wealth and unseen powers lying in the trees, lizards, rocks, and streams all around them.

Rasputin's Codfish Soup

This is the soup that Rasputin always said gave him his health, vigor, and virility. According to his daughter, this was his favorite dish; "Restaurants in Petrograd and Moscow would prepare the concoction whenever they expected Rasputin to dine."

Serves 4

Ingredients:
1 1/2 pounds codfish fillets
3 cups of water
1 cup of milk
1 cup heavy whipping cream
Salt and pepper to taste
1 teaspoon minced ginger
1/2 teaspoon paprika

Method:
Cut fillets into 2 inch pieces and place in saucepan. Add water, milk and whipping cream. Place over medium heat and bring to scalding. Reduce heat and continue simmering until fish is done. Add minced ginger, paprika, salt and pepper to taste.

Entrees

Siberian Pelmeni

Poached Pastries

Pelmeni consist of dough and filling.

Serves 4

Ingredients for the dough:
2 cups wheat flour
1/2 cup water
1 egg
3/4 teaspoon salt

Method:
Sift the flour onto a dough board and make a hollow in the center of the flour. Break in the egg, and add the water and salt. Knead into heavy dough; cover and set aside for half an hour. Roll the dough thin and cut into 2 to 2 1/2 inch rounds. The dough is now ready for the meat filling.

Ingredients for the filling:
1/2 to 1 pound ground beef
1/2 of an onion
Salt and pepper to taste
2/3 cup water
3 cloves of garlic

Method:
Put the garlic and onion through a blender. Transfer to a bowl; add the ground beef, pepper, salt, and water. Mix thoroughly. Put a ball of filling (about the size of a small

walnut) on one half of a dough round and fold over, making a half moon. Pinch the edges; draw the two points together making a little purse.

Lay the pelmeni in 1 gallon of boiling water to which 1 1/2 tablespoons of salt has been added. Continue to boil until the pelmeni rise to the surface. Remove with a skimmer.

Serving suggestion: Tastes great topped with butter, vinegar, sour cream, or mustard.

Tale of Sadko

This tale was written in poetic form by A. Pushkin.

In the fable of Sadko, a man appearing to be a poor psaltery player has talents that are not recognized by the merchants of the City of Novgorod. However, Sadko was very talented. This was the reason that the beautiful Sea Princess, Volkhova, daughter of Tsar Morskoi, the King of the Sea, was charmed by Sandko's music and songs.

One day there was a big feast at a merchant's house. The guests were bragging about their wealth. They asked Sadko to tell them about his wealth. He replied modestly that he was not a rich man, but he knew one secret—there was a magic golden fish in Lake Ilmen that would restore youth to anyone who ate it. The merchants didn't believe him and said that if he caught and ate this fish, they would give him all their goods.

With Princess Volkhova's help he was able to catch the golden fish, and he became one of the richest men in Novgorod. He built a big palace, married a girl named Lubava, and became a prosperous merchant.

On his voyage, Sadko visited Venice, Scandinavia, Egypt, India, and many other countries. But as the ships sailed back to Russia the wind ceased, and the ships could not move. Sadko realized that because the people had not made proper sacrifices to Tsar Morskoi, King of the Sea, the ships now stood still. In order to save the sailors, Sadko sacrificed himself and jumped into the water. Instantly a brisk breeze filled the sails of the ships, and they sailed away towards home.

Sadko fell to the bottom of the sea and found himself in the palace of Tsar Morskoi. The King and Queen of the Sea had heard about Sadko's musical talents and asked him to play and sing for them. They wanted to make Sadko stay in Sea Tsardom, and promised Volkhova to be his bride. But Sadko told Volkhova that he couldn't marry her because he was very much in love with his wife, Lubava. Upset, but willing to help, she snuck him out with the help of a flock of sea horses. They took Sadko back to the shore of Lake Ilmen.

Volkhova sang a lullaby to Sadko and he fell asleep. She then kissed him and disappeared into the mist, becoming the river Volkhova which flows from Lake Ilmen to the sea.

Sadko's wife, Lubava, who was waiting and grieving for her husband all that time, was happy to see her beloved husband again.

Beef Stroganoff

The name of this dish comes from the Russian Count Grigory Stroganove (1770-1857), who was one of the richest noblemen and held the highest diplomatic posts. A great gourmet, he loved delicious dishes and always had the best cooks. One of them invented an original dish from scraped meat and it was a favorite of the Count's. Hence, the dish took the name Stroganoff.

Serves 4

Ingredients:
1 pound beef tenderloin.
Salt and pepper to taste
2 large yellow onions
1/2 pound sour cream
1 tablespoon flour
1 tablespoon butter

Method:
For the sauce, boil 1 cup of water. Add flour, stirring continuously. Boil 10-15 minutes. Add sour cream and salt. Bring back to a boil. Set aside. Chop onions and simmer them with butter at a low temperature for 20 minutes. Add to the sauce. Cut beef into strips 2 inches long by 1/2 inch wide. Add salt and pepper. Thoroughly fry at a high temperature for 10 minutes, and then another 10 minutes at a low temperature. Add the sauce and cook for another 5 minutes.

Serving suggestion: Tastes great served over egg noodles.

Tale of the Fire Bird

In an exotic, far away land, a thief was stealing golden apples from Tsar Berendey's Magic Garden. These golden apples had the power of bestowing youth and beauty. The guards of the tsar were not able to catch him; the thief always got away from them. No one had even seen this thief. The tsar was very angry, since he was married to a beautiful, young queen—he needed the golden apples for himself.

The only person who saw the thief was the tsar's son, Prince Ivan Tsarevich. One night, the young tsarevich hid under a water bucket in the garden, and listened closely to every sound around him. At dawn, the prince almost fell asleep, but the silence was broken by a strange sound. The prince peeked out from under the water bucket so he could see through the thin opening. And he saw the glorious Fire Bird.

In the depth of night the Fire Bird would fly into the garden, its feathers blazing with a silver and golden sheen. Its eyes were shining like diamonds and lit the place as brightly as a million burning fires. The young tsarevich crawled up to the bird and grabbed it by the tail.

The next day Prince Ivan told his father, the tsar, about the Fire Bird. He showed his father one of the Fire Bird's feathers. From that day on, the tsar was obsessed with capturing the Fire Bird for himself. He sent his three sons on a journey to another kingdom to find this remarkable bird.

After a long day's ride, he fell asleep, only to awake in the morning to find his horse gone. Walking through the woods, he met Gray Wolf, who confessed that he ate the horse. Feeling bad about Ivan's situation, Gray Wolf offered to let Ivan ride on his back. Grey Wolf took Ivan to Tsar Afron's kingdom, where

the Fire Bird was being kept in a golden cage inside the tsar's closed off garden. The wolf warned the prince not to take the cage.

The prince snuck in and took the cage, which triggered an alarm. He was captured by Tsar Afron's guards and brought before the Tsar. He was told that in order to have the Fire Bird, he must pay for it with the Horse of the Golden Mane—a possession of Tsar Kusman.

The Gray Wolf carried Ivan to Kusman's palace and advised him to take the horse without the bridle. Once again, the prince didn't listen to the wolf's advice, and took the horse with the bridle. He was captured by Tsar Kusman, who said he would only give the prince the horse in exchange for the fair Princess Elena, who was living with Tsar Dalmat.

This time the wolf decided to do the job himself and stole Princess Elena. He brought her back to Ivan and the prince fell in love with her. The wolf helped trick Kusman by assuming Princess Elena's form. He also tricked Afron by assuming the form of the horse.

When Ivan returned with Princess Elena, the Horse of the Golden Mane, and the Fire Bird, his two brothers couldn't believe their eyes. They became envious of him and decided to kill him. Once the wolf learned of what had happened, he went on a search for the Waters of Life and Death.

The wolf returned and splashed the prince with the Waters of Life and Death, which revived him. Ivan Tsarevich went back to his father, the tsar, and told him about the events. The tsar angrily banished his two sons.

Ivan Tsarevich married Elena the Fair and they lived happily ever after.

Chicken Kiev

This juicy, tender chicken dish is sure to have the diners asking for seconds.

Serves 4

Ingredients:
2 cups butter
6 cloves garlic, diced
1/2 cup lemon juice
4 chicken breasts
4 eggs
Salt, pepper, and paprika to taste
1 1/2 cups scallions, finely diced
6 cups breadcrumbs
1 1/2 cups Parmesan cheese, grated

Method:
In a frying pan, melt the butter and sauté garlic with lemon juice. Add salt, pepper, and paprika. Using a marinade injector, inject the breasts with some of the butter mix. Add remaining liquid to eggs and beat. In a separate bowl, combine scallions, breadcrumbs, and Parmesan cheese. Dip the breasts in the egg mixture and then coat in the bread crumb mixture. Bake at 350 degrees F for 45 minutes.

Serving suggestion: Serve with Grechnevaya Kasha (Buckwheat with Mushrooms and Onions). See recipe on page 118.

Tale of the Twelve Months

Everyone in the world knows that there are twelve months in a year, that each month follows the last, and that they never meet. But legend says that long ago there was a little girl who saw all twelve months at one time!

In a small village there lived a greedy and wicked woman who loved her own daughter, but hated her well mannered, hardworking stepdaughter. The stepdaughter didn't even have time to rest. She brought heavy pails of water, gathered wood in the forest, laundered, and weeded the garden. The poor girl worked every day, no matter what the weather was like outside. Perhaps that was why she was so lucky to see all twelve months at the same time.

One day in January, there was so much snow that no one dared to go outside. In the evening, though, the greedy woman sent her poor stepdaughter to the forest to pick snowdrops for her stepsister's birthday.

"But the snowdrops won't be blooming for another two months—at least!" cried the poor girl.

Her stepmother said, "I don't want to hear about it. Go out there and find them, and don't come back until you do."

Since the girl had no choice, she went out in the cold winter night and started walking through the frozen woods. She walked farther and farther and got colder and colder, but there wasn't a living thing to be seen. The wind began to blow and the snow began to fall.

Suddenly she saw a light in the distance. As she walked slowly toward the light, it became brighter and clearer. There was a campfire in the middle of the clearing. There were 12 men of varying ages: three of the men were old, three were middle-aged, three were young men, and the last three were boys. They were sitting around the fire and talking. The men were beautifully dressed. One of the men saw the girl and asked "Who are you? Where have you come from, and what do you want here?"

She bowed politely to them and told them that her stepmother had ordered her to pick snowdrops for her stepsister. The old man laughed. "This must be a joke! Snowdrops don't grow in January!"

The little girl replied, "I was sent here by my stepmother who told me that I must fill the basket with snowdrops or else never return home."

The twelve men took pity on her and decided to help. Suddenly one of the young men, with a fur cape on one shoulder, came to the oldest man and said to him, "Let me take your place for few minutes, brother January."

January, the eldest, then struck his stave into the ground. Everything around them became quiet; the snowflakes began to fall on the ground. He turned to February and said, "It is now your turn, brother February," and stepped aside.

February struck the ground with his stave; the wind began to blow and a snowstorm began. He turned to March and said, "Now it is your turn."

Snowdrifts and icicles disappeared completely. Fresh green leaves burst out on the branches of the trees around them, and flowers started blooming. The little girl stood there, mesmerized.

She picked a full basket of snowdrops, and then she filled her apron as well with the small, fragrant flowers. She ran back to the glade and thanked each month in turn, before she ran home.

When she returned home and told what had happened to her

in the forest, the jealous stepmother let her own daughter go to the glade to ask the twelve months for berries, mushrooms, apples and cucumbers. The girl found the glade and the twelve months around the big fire. But this daughter was rude to them and did not get anything. January waved his hand and she was buried in thick layers of snow. Her mother tried to find her, but also was frozen to death.

The kindhearted stepdaughter lived long and happily. In May, she had the freshest flowers in her house, in June the best berries, and in September the best apples. In the winter, the worst of the storms and blizzards seemed to miss her house. People said that the twelve months visited her regularly and always gave her their blessings.

Chicken Gorky

This gourmet delight will add flavor to your chicken.

Serves 6

Ingredients:
6 chicken breasts
2 ounces vodka, heated
1 tablespoon tomato paste
5 tablespoons butter
1 tablespoon flour
1 1/2 cups sour cream or plain yogurt
4 tablespoons feta cheese, crumbled
Salt and pepper to taste
2 tablespoons dried parsley
1 garlic clove, minced
3/4 cup chicken broth
1/4 cup onion chopped

Method:
Sauté the chicken breasts and onions with butter in a frying pan. Pour heated vodka over the chicken and onions. Add the garlic, salt, pepper, and parsley. Remove chicken from the pan and dip in flour. Add the tomato paste and chicken broth to the pan. Stir in the sour cream and feta cheese. Bring to a boil, stirring constantly. Add the chicken back to the mixture, reduce heat, and simmer for 20 to 30 minutes. Arrange the chicken in a deep casserole dish. Pour the mixture over the chicken and cook in preheated 350 degree F oven for 20 minutes or until brown on top.

The Tale of the Golden Cockerel

This is one of many great works by Alexander Pushkin.

Tsar Dadon was a proud and bellicose ruler. When he was young, he conquered neighboring kingdoms and was infamous throughout the land. With age he grew weaker and wanted to live peacefully. His enemies, sensing his weakness, planned attacks on his rich kingdom. He offered a great reward in return for finding a perfect security system. No one could find a secure technique. Just when the tsar started to get frustrated there appeared an astrologer who told him that he had the answer. The astrologer gave him a Golden Cockerel. The Cockerel, sitting on a spire atop Dadon's palace, would crow loudly in warning if enemies approached. The tsar was very pleased with the magician's gift and promised to grant him any reward he desired.

The magic Cockerel guarded Tsar Dadon's kingdom effectively. One day, the Cockerel crowed more loudly then ever. There was an enemy army advancing towards Tsar Dadon's land. The tsar sent his elder son and his mighty army to fight the enemy. The kingdom was saved, but the tsar's son and army never returned.

The Cockerel cried out again, and the tsar sent out more troops—this time led by his younger son. The son and the army didn't return.

The Cockerel then crowed for the third time, sounding the alarm that another army was planning to invade. This time, Dadon himself led an army to the borders of the kingdom. After several days' march, he came upon a terrible battlefield where both of his armies and his two sons lay slain. Tsar Dadon was overcome with grief. He saw a tent and walked in to sit down, and there his sorrow was lifted when he saw a woman of great beauty! Before him stood the seductive Queen of Shemakha. Dadon was bewitched by her and planned to marry her once they returned to his castle. But on the way home they encountered the Astrologer who asked the tsar to pay for the Golden Cockerel by giving him the Queen of Shemakha. Infuriated, Dadon hit the magician with his staff, killing him.

The Golden Cockerel then flew down from his spire and pecked Dadon to death for not keeping his end of the bargain.

Chicken Tabaka

Serves 6

Ingredients:
2 Cornish hens
6 garlic cloves, crushed
4 tablespoon butter
Salt and pepper to taste
Cayenne and paprika to taste

Method:
Pat hens dry and place them breast side up on a large cutting board. Cut down the middle of the breastbone using a sharp knife to separate the rib cage. Turn hens over and flatten them with a mallet. With a sharp knife, poke small holes all over the hens. Insert some garlic into the holes. Rub the hens with the rest of the crushed garlic, salt, and pepper. Then dust with cayenne and paprika.

Heat a large cast-iron skillet. Add butter. When the butter is melted put hens in the pan, turning to coat both sides. Cook skin side up over medium high heat for 5 minutes. Then turn skin side down. Place a flat cover or plate over hens and weigh them down with a heavy can or bowl filled with water. Cook hens over medium heat for 20 minutes or until the skin is brown and slightly crusty. Turn, replace weight, and cook for another 5 minutes

Serving suggestion: For the best taste serve straight out of the skillet.

Tale of the Golden Haired Girl

Many years ago, in a land far away, there was a great magician named Poloza who was the keeper of the Ural Mountains' treasures. Poloza had many guards who watched over all his gold, silver, and jewels. He had a beautiful daughter named Golden Hair. One day a handsome hunter from the Bashkirian tribe was hunting near their palace. Golden Hair saw him and instantly knew that she had to meet him. Soon after, they fell in love and wanted to get married. Their plan was to go live in the hunter's house.

Poloza did not want to hear any of it and refused to allow the marriage to take place. Not wanting to be apart from each other, the young hunter abducted Golden Hair. But Poloza was able to bring his daughter back to the palace.

The young hunter was heartbroken and went to seek advice from the magic wise owl who lived deep in the forest. The owl told him that the only place where Poloza's magical powers could not reach was a large island located in the middle of the Lake. However, the hunter and the Golden Haired Girl would have to stay on this island for eternity.

Once again, the young hunter abducted the Golden Haired Girl from her father's palace and t her to the island in the middle of the lake. This time the magic powers of Poloza were useless in taking his daughter away from the hunter.

The island turned out to be the couple's paradise. It had meadows and forests, herds of horses and sheep, great big gardens with flowers in bloom all year round, and plenty of food.

Many centuries have passed, and legend has it that sometimes at dawn, couples walking along the bank of the lake can see the island and a mysterious maiden sitting on a stone at the water's edge. She lets her hair down, and the water turns into pure gold.

Chicken Kotleti

Chicken Patties

Serves 8

Ingredients:
2 pounds ground chicken
2 cups breadcrumbs
1/2 cup light cream
1 egg, lightly beaten
Salt and pepper to taste
Cayenne pepper to taste
Nutmeg to taste
4 tablespoons butter
1 tablespoon vegetable oil
1/4 cup scallions, finely chopped
2/3 cup whipping cream
2 tablespoon white vinegar
2/3 cup sour cream

Method:
In a large bowl, mix together 1 cup of the breadcrumbs and the cream. Combine with the chicken, egg, salt, and a pinch each of the cayenne, nutmeg, and pepper. Spread remaining crumbs in a shallow pan. Divide chicken mixture into 8 portions. With wet hands, form each portion into a round patty. Flatten slightly in center. Gently roll each patty in breadcrumbs and place on a waxed paper-lined tray. In a large skillet, heat 1 tablespoon of butter and the oil. Arrange patties in a single layer and sauté over medium heat for about 5 minutes on each side until patties are golden brown. For the sauce, melt the

remaining 3 tablespoons of butter in a small saucepan, and cook scallions, without browning, for 3 minutes. Add the cream. Increase the heat to high and cook, stirring constantly, until cream thickens slightly.

Serving suggestion: Serve the cream in a separate bowl from the patties. Each diner can pour the sauce over the patties. Tastes great with Grechnavaya Kasha; recipe on page 118.

Tale of the Princess Frog

Once upon a time, in a far away land, the tsar decided that it was time for his three sons to get married. He ordered them to shoot their arrows, and whichever maiden lived where their arrows should land would be their bride. The eldest son drew back his bow and shot his arrow. It landed in the courtyard of a nobleman's daughter. The middle son then drew his bow and shot his arrow. It landed in the courtyard of a merchant's daughter. The youngest son, Ivan, drew back his bow and shot his arrow, and it landed in a swamp.

Ivan walked to the swamp and found a frog next to his arrow. The frog spoke to him in a human voice and told him that he would not regret marrying her. Ivan brought the frog to his father's palace. His two brothers laughed at him, and Ivan implored the tsar not to make him marry the frog. But the tsar stood firmly by his order, and Ivan and the frog were married.

Soon after his sons were married, the tsar ordered his daughters-in-law to make him fine shirts and bake him tasty bread. Ivan expressed his concern to the frog, and she replied for him not to worry and sent Ivan to bed. Once Ivan was asleep, the frog removed her skin and turned into Vasilisa the Beautiful. She stood in the doorway, clapped her hands, and her servants came running to her aid. When Ivan woke up the next morning, the frog handed a loaf of freshly baked white bread and a dressy shirt to him. After tasting the bread of all three wives, the tsar declared that the bread of Ivan's wife was by far the best. After trying on all of the shirts, the tsar liked the one that Ivan's wife made the most.

The tsar then announced a feast at the palace and ordered his sons to come with their wives. There for the first time Vasilisa

114

the Beautiful appeared for everyone to see, including her husband Ivan. Later at the dance, Vasilisa performed magical feats with the wave of her sleeves. The wives of the other sons tried to do the same, but to no avail.

Ivan was so taken with her and wanted her to remain a beautiful princess that he snuck back to their home and destroyed her frog skin. Vasilisa screamed at him to stop, but it was too late. As soon as her skin was destroyed, Vasilisa disappeared and became a prisoner of Koschei the Deathless—thus was her curse.

Ivan set out on a journey into the woods to seek out Baba Yaga, a witch. The witch gave him advice on how to get Vasilisa the Beautiful back. Baba Yaga told him that the only way he could free his wife was by killing Koschei. In order to do that, he had to travel to the Island of Buyan. Koshchei's death was well hidden at the point of a needle, the needle hidden in an egg, the egg in a duck, the duck in a rabbit, and the rabbit in a chest at the top of an oak tree.

Ivan climbed the oak tree, snapped the needle, and freed Vasilisa. They returned to their home and lived happily ever after.

Grechnevaya Kasha

Buckwheat with Mushrooms and Onions

Serves 6

Ingredients:
1 cup of coarse buckwheat
1 egg
1 teaspoon of salt
8 tablespoons of butter
3 cups of boiling water
2 cups onions, finely chopped
1/2 pound fresh mushrooms, finely chopped

Method:
In a mixing bowl, mix the buckwheat and egg with a large wooden spoon until the grains are thoroughly coated. Transfer to a skillet and cook uncovered over medium heat, stirring constantly, until the buckwheat is lightly toasted and dry. Add the salt, 3 tablespoons of butter, and 2 cups of boiling water. Stir thoroughly, cover the pan, and reduce the heat to low. Cook for about 20 minutes, stirring occasionally. If at this point the buckwheat is not yet tender and seems dry, stir in the additional cup of boiling water and cook covered 10 minutes longer or until the water is absorbed and the grains are separate and fluffy. Remove the pan from the heat.

Meanwhile, melt 3 tablespoons of butter in a skillet over high heat. Lower the heat to medium, and add the chopped onions. Stirring frequently, fry for 3 to 4 minutes or until the onions are soft and golden. Stir the onions into the buckwheat. Melt the remaining 2 tablespoons of butter in the skillet over high heat. Stir in the mushrooms, reduce the heat, and cook for 3 minutes, stirring frequently. Then raise the heat to high, and cook the mushrooms uncovered until all the liquid has evaporated. Add the mushrooms to the buckwheat and onions and toss together. Season to taste.

Serving suggestion: This delicious dish can be served alone or with one of the chicken dishes included earlier.

Tale of Sivka-Burka

Once upon a time there lived an old peasant who had three sons. The two older brothers were smart and handsome, but the youngest was a fool named Ivan. One day the peasant discovered something was trampling his wheat field at night. He requested that the oldest brother keep watch one night so that he could catch the culprit. The oldest brother stood watch that night, but fell asleep. It was then the middle brother's turn, and he fell asleep as well. The peasant had no choice but to ask the youngest one. Ivan stood up all night and saw the most beautiful chestnut-grey stallion with a gold saddle and silver bridle. Ivan caught the horse and was about to bring him to his father when the horse spoke. He told Ivan that if he let him go, he would help fulfill his wishes. He said, "When you need me, come to the field, whistle, and call 'Sivka-Burka, appear!'" Ivan agreed and let the horse go free.

Meanwhile, the tsar was seeking a husband for his daughter. He decided that the young man who could accomplish a difficult task would be worthy of his daughter's hand in marriage. He placed his daughter in a high tower and announced that if someone on horseback could jump high enough to take the ring from her finger, he could marry the princess. Ivan summoned Sivka- Burka, who turned him into a handsome young prince, and they galloped off to the tsar's courtyard.

Ivan reached the princess and took the ring from her finger. But he galloped off so quickly that nobody saw his face. At home he turned back into the fool, Ivan, and bandaged one hand, telling his brothers that he had injured himself.

The next day there was a big feast at the tsar's palace.

Everyone in the land was invited, and Ivan's family went. At the end of the feast the princess served everyone honey. She saw the bandage on Ivan's hand and asked him to untie it. He removed the bandage, and in his hand was her ring for all to see. Once again Ivan summoned Sivka-Burka to turn him into a handsome prince, and he married the beautiful princess.

Golubtsy
Stuffed Cabbage Rolls in Sour Cream Sauce

Serves 6

Ingredients:
1 3-pound head white cabbage
3 cups onions, finely chopped
12 tablespoons of butter (1 1/2 quarter-pound sticks)
1/4 pound ground beef
1/4 cup unconverted long grain rice
Salt and black pepper to taste
2 tablespoons vegetable oil
3 large tomatoes, peeled, seeded, and chopped
1 tablespoon flour
1/2 cup sour cream
1/4 cup fresh dill leaves for garnish, finely cut

Method:
Drop the cabbage into a large pot of boiling water and let it cook for 10 minutes. Remove the cabbage (letting the water continue to boil) and carefully detach as many of the outer leave as you can. Return the cabbage to the boiling water and cook for a few minutes longer. Remove, and again detach as many leaves as you can. Repeat this process until the whole cabbage has been separated into individual leaves. Discard the smaller inner leaves.

Bring 2 cups of water to a boil in a saucepan. Add the rice, and boil, uncovered, for about 12 minutes. Drain and set aside.

In a skillet, melt 4 tablespoons of butter. Add 2 cups of onions, and cook, stirring occasionally, 8 to 10 minutes or until they are soft and lightly browned. Transfer them to a large mixing bowl. Add the ground meat, rice, salt, and pepper. Mix together until well combined. Lay the cabbage leaves side by side, and with a small knife trim the base of each leaf of its rough rib end. Place 1/2 cup of the filling in the center of each of the 12 largest leaves, and roll up all of the leaves tightly, neatly tucking in the ends as if you were wrapping a package.

Preheat the oven to 325 degrees F. In a skillet, melt 4 tablespoons of the butter in the 2 tablespoons of oil over high heat. When the foam begins to subside, add 4 to 6 cabbage rolls, seam-sides down, and fry 3 to 5 minutes on each side or until golden brown. Transfer the rolls to a shallow baking dish just large enough to hold them in one layer, and proceed to brown the remaining rolls.

Melt the remaining 4 tablespoons of butter in the skillet, and add the remaining cup of chopped onions. Cook 3 to 4 minutes or until the onions are soft and translucent, then stir in the chopped tomatoes, salt, and pepper. In a small mixing bowl, beat the flour into the sour cream one teaspoon at a time. Stir the mixture into the tomatoes and onions. Season to taste, and pour the sauce over the cabbage rolls, masking them completely. Bake uncovered in the center of the oven for 45 minutes or until the rolls are golden brown.

Serving suggestion: Sprinkle with chopped dill and serve hot.

Tale of Alyonushka

Once there lived an old man and his wife. They had a daughter named Alyonushka and a small son named Ivanushka.

The old man and the old woman died, and Alyonushka and Ivanushka were left all alone in the world. Alyonushka set off to work, and took her little brother with her. They had a long way to go, and after they had been walking for a time, Ivanushka began to feel very thirsty.

"Sister Alyonushka, I am thirsty," he said.

"Be patient, we shall soon come to a well."

They continued walking and the sun was now high up in the sky. They came upon a cow's hoof filled with water, and Ivanushka said, "May I drink out of the hoof?"

"No, little brother. If you do, you will turn into a calf."

Ivanushka listened to his sister, and they walked on. The sun was still high up in the sky, and the heat was so unbearable that they felt weak. They came upon a horse's hoof filled with water, and Ivanushka asked, "May I drink out of the hoof, Alyonushka?"

"No, little brother. If you do, you will turn into a foal."

Ivanushka obeyed and they walked on. They came upon a goat's hoof filled with water, and Ivanushka asked, "May I drink from it?"

Alyonushka once again answered, "No, if you do you will turn into a kid."

But this time the boy didn't listen to his sister's warning, and after taking his first sip he turned into a small goat.

Alyonushka started to cry. She was sobbing on the ground by a stack of hay while the little goat skipped 'round in play. Just then a Merchant was riding by.

"Why are you crying?" he asked. Alyonushka told him of the events. The merchant asked her to marry him. He promised to dress her in gold and silver, and the little goat would live with them.

Alyonushka thought it over and agreed to marry the Merchant.

They lived together happily, and the little goat lived with them. He ate and drank with Alyonushka out of the same cup.

One day the Merchant went away from home, and all of a sudden a witch appeared. She stood under Alyonushka's window and begged her ever so sweetly to go bathe in the river with her. Alyonushka followed the witch to the river. But when they got there, the witch attacked her, tied a stone round her neck, and threw her into the water. The witch then took on Alyonushka's shape.

Only poor Ivanushka knew the truth about his sister. Little did he know that the witch was planning to get rid of him, too. After overhearing him one day as he talked to his sister in the lake, she told the merchant to kill the little goat.

The merchant didn't have the heart to kill Ivanushka, as he loved the goat like a person. But, being deceived by the witch, he felt his wife's wishes to be the most important. Ivanushka asked the merchant if he could go to the river for one last drink before he died, and the merchant agreed. At the river's edge the goat screamed out to his sister, and she answered him that she couldn't help him since there was a stone tied around her neck. A peasant was passing by and heard their conversation. The peasant went to the merchant and told him what he had witnessed.

Upon hearing the peasant's story, the merchant ran to the river, found Alyonushka, and removed the stone from around her neck. Alyonushka emerged from the river even more beautiful than before. The witch was then tied to a horse that was then turned loose in an open field. The little goat was so happy that he turned three somersaults, and was changed back into a boy.

They lived happily ever after.

Osetrina

Sturgeon or Halibut in Tomato and Mushroom Sauce

Serves 8

Ingredients:
2 cups onions, thinly sliced
1 bay leaf
1/4 cup carrots, peeled and coarsely chopped
1/2 parsley root, coarsely chopped
4 large tomatoes, peeled, seeded, and coarsely chopped
5 tablespoons butter
4 cups cold water
1 1/2 pounds fresh sturgeon or halibut steaks
1/2 cup fresh mushrooms, thinly sliced
1/2 cup heavy cream

Method:
Preheat the oven to 200 degrees F. In a 4-quart casserole, combine the onions, bay leaf, carrots, parsley root, tomatoes, 3 tablespoons of butter, and 4 cups of cold water. Bring to a boil over high heat, stirring constantly. Then reduce the heat to medium, partially cover the casserole, and simmer for 30 minutes. Pour the entire contents of the casserole into a fine sieve over a large bowl. Press down on the vegetables with the back of a large spoon to extract all of their juices before discarding them.

Return the strained stock to the casserole, add fish, and bring to a boil over high heat. Immediately reduce the heat to low, cover the casserole, and simmer 6 to 8 minutes or until the fish is opaque and firm to the touch. Be careful not to overcook.

Transfer the fish to a deep oven-proof serving dish, and cover it with foil.

Bring the stock back to a boil over high heat, and continue to boil, uncovered, until it has cooked down to about 1 1/2 cups. Melt the 2 remaining tablespoons of butter in a skillet over high heat, and add the mushrooms. Reduce the heat to medium, and cook for 5 minutes, stirring the mushrooms occasionally, until they are soft and most of the juices have evaporated. Stir in the reduced stock and turn off the heat. Beat in the heavy cream, 1 tablespoon at a time. Pour the sauce over the fish before serving.

Tale of the Golden Fish

This is one of Alexander Pushkin's well known poems.

Once upon a time, a peasant couple lived in a shack close to the edge of the sea. The old man caught fish in the sea and made a living by selling it to merchants. One morning, while he was fishing, something glittery caught his eye. He looked down into his net and saw that he had caught the Golden Fish.

To his utter amazement the Golden Fish started speaking to him in human voice. The fish asked to be thrown back into the sea, and in return the old man would be granted wishes. But the kindhearted fisherman didn't ask for anything, and returned the Golden Fish to the sea. The old man home and told his wife about this amazing fish that he caught. She was furious with him for not asking anything in return. She told him to go back, catch the Golden Fish, and wish for a gourmet dinner to be on their table. The fisherman did as she asked of him—he caught the fish and wished for a gourmet dinner on his table. When he came home, he found the table to be full of delicious food.

The fisherman's wife became greedier and decided that she wanted more than just a dinner. The next morning she sent her husband to ask for a new washtub. He returned home to find his wife standing next to a new washtub, but she still wasn't satisfied.

The following day she demanded that the husband go to the sea to find the Golden Fish and wish for a new house. The old man came home to find his wife standing next to the new house. But the wife wanted more now, and the fisherman was sent back again the next day to wish for his wife to become a noblewoman with a bigger, newer house.

This time when the old man came up to the edge of the sea, the water was turbulent and waves were rolling in. He asked the fish to make his wife a noblewoman and to make the house much bigger. He returned home to find his wife dressed in riches and servants hovering around her. But she was still unhappy and demanded to become Queen of all the land.

The fisherman was embarrassed to go back and ask the Golden Fish for this wish. He came to the edge of the sea and with his head bowed low he asked the fish to make his wife the Queen of all the land. This, too, didn't satisfy her. She sent her husband one last time to the sea to catch the Golden Fish to wish that she would be ruler of the sea and of all creatures who live in it and to rule over the Golden Fish.

Once the fisherman approached the sea, it was more turbulent then ever with the waves crashing all around. The old man caught the fish and made the wish. The fish told him to go home and he would find what his wife deserves. When he returned home, his wife was dressed in old rags, standing by her old broken washtub, inside the old shack. The fisherman never caught the Golden Fish again.

Zharkoye

Beef Stew

This is a very tasty, aromatic, ancient Russian dish.

Serves 6

Ingredients:
12 ounces beef
5 potatoes
1 onion
5 cups water
2 tablespoons butter
1 carrot
1 parsley root
1 celery root
2 garlic cloves
2 tablespoons green dill and parsley, chopped
Salt and black pepper to taste

Method:
Melt the butter in a large skillet. Slice the onion. Sauté the onions in the skillet until they are golden brown. Chop the garlic and add one of the cloves to the onions. Cut carrot into small cubes and add them to the skillet. Cube beef and fry in butter until light brown. Add the other chopped garlic clove, chopped roots, dill and parsley, and season with salt and pepper. Add water and stir. Peel, wash, and cut the potatoes into medium size cubes and immerse them into the broth. Cover and cook for 30 minutes or until the potatoes are tender.

Desserts

Desserts are traditionally served with tea brewed in a Samovar. Preserves (or jam) are placed on the table, and each diner places a few teaspoonfuls of the preserves into their tea as a substitute for sugar.

Koloby

Sweet Dough Balls

Ingredients:
3 cups barley flour
2 eggs
1 cup sour cream
2 tablespoons oil
1 cup sugar
Salt to taste

Method:
Combine all of the ingredients to form dough. Knead dough and roll out to 2 inches thick. Make rounds with a small glass, and put them on a greased baking sheet. Bake at 450 degrees F about 30 minutes or until light brown.

Tale of Kolobok

A kolobok is a round bun, which is made from dough. Children especially love this treat with their glass of milk.

Once upon a time, there lived an old man and an old woman who were very poor. One day they had nothing left to eat in the house, not even bread. The old man said to his wife, "Bake us a bun! If you scrape out the flour box and sweep out the bin, you'll have enough flour."

The old woman scraped out the flour box and swept out the bin, made some dough, and shaped a little round bun out of it. She then baked the bun in the oven and put it on the window sill to cool. But the bun rolled out of the window, onto the bench outside, and from the bench onto the ground, and away it rolled along the road!

The kolobok rolled down the road until it met a rabbit.

"Kolobok, kolobok, I'll eat you now."

"Don't eat me until after I sing you a song—

"I'm kolobok, kolobok!
I was scraped up in the flour tin,
Swept up from the bin,
Baked in the oven till I was done,
Then sat on the sill and rolled down.
I ran away from grandmother,
I ran away from grandfather too,
and now I will be on my way running from you."

Kolobok quickly rolled off, away from the rabbit.

The kolobok rolled down the road until it bumped into a wolf.

"Kolobok, kolobok, I'll eat you now."
"Don't eat me until after I sing you a song—

"I'm kolobok, kolobok!
I was scraped up in the flour tin,
Swept up from the bin,
Baked in the oven till I was done,
Then sat on the sill and rolled down.
I ran away from grandmother,
I ran away from grandfather,
I ran away from the rabbit too,
and now I will be on my way running from you."

It rolled down the road so fast that the wolf couldn't catch it.
The kolobok rolled down the road until it met a bear.
"Kolobok, kolobok, I'll eat you now."
"Don't eat me until after I sing you a song—

"I'm kolobok, kolobok!
I was scraped up in the flour tin,
Swept up from the bin,
Baked in the oven till I was done,
Then sat on the sill and rolled down.
I ran away from grandmother,
I ran away from grandfather,
I ran away from the rabbit,
I ran away from the wolf too,
and now I will be on my way running from you."

Again it rolled off down the road, so fast that the bear couldn't catch it.
The kolobok rolled down the road until it bumped into a fox.

"Kolobok, kolobok, where are you going?"
"I'm just rolling down the road."
"Kolobok, kolobok, I'll eat you now."
"Don't eat me until after I sing you a song—

"I'm kolobok, kolobok!
I was scraped up in the flour-tin,
Swept up from the bin,
Baked in the oven till I was done,
Then sat on the sill and rolled down.
I ran away from grandmother,
I ran away from grandfather,
I ran away from the rabbit,
I ran away from the wolf too,
and now, Fox I will be on my way running from you."

But the sly fox said, "What a nice song. But I am rather hard of hearing. Could you please sit on my nose and sing your song again, a little louder."

The kolobok rolled onto the fox's nose and sang the song again a little louder.

But the fox said, "Kolobok. Please sit on my tongue and sing your song just one more time."

As soon as the kolobok rolled onto the fox's tongue, the fox gobbled it up.

Ponchiki

Doughnuts

This Russian dessert will give new meaning to doughnuts.

Ingredients:
1 1/2 cups flour
2 tablespoons sugar
1 tablespoon butter
1 egg
1/2 cup milk
1/2 teaspoon baking powder
1/2 cup peanut oil
Ground cinnamon to taste
Powdered sugar

Method:
Add cinnamon and baking powder to flour. Sift it into a bowl. Beat egg with sugar, add butter, and then mix in milk. While stirring, gradually the flour mixture. Knead to a stiff dough. Roll out dough 1/2 inch thick. Make rounds with a cup, and then make rounds within the rounds using a cup with a smaller diameter, forming rings. In a frying pan, put 2 to 3 rings at a time in hot oil, and fry until light golden. Remove and sprinkle baked doughnuts with powdered sugar.

Tale of the Crystal Lake

In a far away kingdom, there once lived a wealthy landowner who had many servants. He was greedy and demanding. One of the servants, Ivan, was a very skilled hunter.

One day, the landowner demanded that Ivan bring him something different than usual from his hunt. Ivan set out deep into the woods. After many hours of walking, he heard the sound of water rippling behind a large tree. Ivan walked closer and saw the most beautiful sight. It was a lake—a lake so clear and serene that it appeared to be made out of crystal. He called it Crystal Lake.

On this Crystal Lake there were twelve snow- white swans floating on the surface of the water. Ivan was so captivated by the beauty of these graceful birds that there was no way he intended to hunt and capture any of them. He came back to the landowner empty-handed. The landowner ordered that Ivan be whipped as punishment for not doing his duty. Strangely, Ivan did not feel the pain of this whipping. All he could think about and see were the twelve beautiful swans.

The next day the greedy landowner ordered Ivan to go hunt. Ivan went straight to the Crystal Lake, although he knew that he would not hunt. He reached the Crystal Lake and hid behind a large boulder. Soon after, the twelve snow-white swans flew down from the cloudless blue sky and began splashing and playing on the water. Ivan was amazed by the swans' beauty yet again and couldn't complete the hunt. He came back to the landowner empty-handed. The landowner once again punished Ivan, keeping him locked in a tiny shed for three whole days and nights! The memory of the graceful swans kept Ivan from losing hope.

After he was released from the shed, the landowner sent him to go hunt. Ivan was drawn back to the Crystal Lake, so that he could have another glimpse of the swans. He went to the lake and hid behind the big boulder. The swans appeared again. As soon as they touched the ground, the swans turned into beautiful maidens. The youngest maiden was the most beautiful of them all. The maidens began singing and dancing around in a circle. Ivan was very surprised; he had never seen such exquisite beauty. After finishing the dance, the maidens disrobed and went for a swim in the lake. Ivan crawled up to their clothes and took the shoes that belonged to the youngest maiden.

When the maidens came out from the lake, they put their clothes back on, turned into white swans, and quickly flew away. But the youngest maiden could not find her shoes and therefore had to stay. She stood on a rock and announced, "Who will return my shoes? If you are an old man, I will respect you as I would a father. If you are younger than I, you shall be my sworn brother. And if we are the same age, you shall be my groom."

Ivan knew that if he was to return to the wealthy landowner he would be punished. He stepped out from his hiding place and revealed himself. The young maiden was impressed with Ivan's bravery. They were married and went to live at her father's kingdom. Ivan's life as a servant was over. The greedy landowner waited many years for Ivan to return.

Gozinakh

Walnut Honey Candy

Ingredients:
1 pound shelled walnuts, finely chopped
2 cups honey
6 tablespoons sugar

Method:
Preheat oven to 350 degrees F. Spread the chopped nuts in a single layer in a pan and toast them in the oven for 10 minutes, turning them over with a spoon from time to time. In a heavy 2-quart pan, combine the honey and sugar and bring to a boil, stirring constantly. Lower the heat and stir in the nuts. Stirring often, cook for 15 minutes. Brush the inside of an 8 to 9 inch round pan with cold water and pour in the nut mixture. Smooth the top and set aside, uncovered, to cool. When firm, dip the pan into hot water and invert a flat plate on top. Grasping the two firmly together, turn over— the candy should slide out in one piece. With a sharp knife dipped in hot water, cut into square shapes.

Serving suggestion: Goes great with unsweetened black tea.

Tale of Havroshechka

This tale was written by Alexander Afanasiev, who wrote some of the best Russian tales around the middle of the nineteenth century.

A girl by the name of Havroshechka was orphaned at a very young age. She went to live with a mean woman who had three daughters—One-Eye, Two-Eyes, and Three-Eyes. Poor Havroshechka was made to do all of the work while the woman and the daughters sat around all day with their hands folded. They constantly bossed the girl around. The only comfort Havroshechka found was in telling all of her troubles to an old cow in the field behind the house. Hearing the complaints about the amount of work that she had to do, the cow told her to jump into one of her ears and climb out the other, and all the work would be done for her. Havroshechka jumped into one of the cow's ears and out the other, and just as the cow promised, all the work had been finished.

The evil woman became suspicious of how quickly Havroshachka was getting her work completed. She told One-Eye to follow Havroshechka and watch every move she made. They went to the fields, and One-Eye, being lazy, laid down to rest. "Sleep little eye!" whispered Havroshechka. Once the girl fell asleep, Havroshechka climbed into the cow's ear and out the other and her work was done. One-Eye went home and was scolded for falling asleep and not watching over Havroshechka.

The next day, Two-Eye was sent to the fields, and being very lazy, she too laid down. "Sleep one eye, sleep other eye!" whispered Havroshechka, who then ran off to the cow. The woman scolded her second daughter for not being awake to

watch over Havroshechka. The next day she sent Three-Eye.

The two girls went to the fields, and growing tired, Three-Eyes laid down to rest. "Sleep one eye, sleep other eye!" said Havroshechka. But she forgot about the girl's third eye, which saw everything. Three-Eyes went back to her mother and told her the story, and the woman immediately ordered that the cow be killed. Before it's death, the cow told Havroshechka to take its bones, wrap them in a kerchief, bury them in the garden, and water them every day. She did as the cow instructed her, and a beautiful apple tree grew in that spot.

One day, a handsome prince was riding by. He saw the four girls out in front of the house and then saw the apple tree. He said, "Whoever brings me an apple from that tree I will take as my bride." Instantly the three daughters began pushing each other aside as they tried to grab an apple, but the tree raised its branches high out of reach and shook its leaves down into the faces of the girls. When Havroshechka came over to the tree, it lowered its branches within her reach, and she picked a juicy, sweet apple and handed it to the prince. As promised, he married her and took her away from the mean family to live happily ever after. Havroshechka never forgot the kind old cow.

Russian Stuffed Pumpkin

This will look great on the holiday table.

Ingredients:
1 4-pound pumpkin
1 1/2 cups long grain rice
2 large tart cooking apples, peeled, cored, and diced
1/2 cup golden raisins
1/2 cup dried sour cherries
8 tablespoons (1 stick) unsalted butter, melted
1 tablespoon sugar
3/4 teaspoon ground cinnamon
Salt to taste
1/4 cup hot water

Method:
Cut the stem end of the pumpkin and set aside the "lid".
Remove the insides of pumpkin, and using a knife or melon
baller, scoop out the flesh of the pumpkin—as much as you can
without piercing the skin. Chop flesh and set aside. In a large
saucepan, bring 3 quarts of salted water to a boil and dump in
the rice. Cover and cook over high heat for about 15 minutes.
Drain well. Preheat oven to 325 degrees F. In a large bowl,
combine the pumpkin flesh, partially cooked rice, raisins, dried
sour cherries, and melted butter. Add the sugar, salt and
cinnamon. Spoon stuffing into the pumpkin, sprinkle with the
hot water and put the "lid" on tightly. Place on a baking sheet
and bake for 2 hours, till pumpkin is tender.

Serving suggestion: Cut into wedges and serve.

Tale of the Wooden Eagle

Once upon a time in a kingdom far away, there lived a tsar. He had many servants, gunsmiths, goldsmiths, cooks, and many others who served him. The tsar liked beautiful carvings and adornments. Every day, all of the court masters gathered in the yard to find out what new task the tsar had concocted for them to accomplish. One day, an argument erupted between a joiner and a goldsmith about which of them was the best in his profession and whose job was more difficult.

The tsar heard their conversation, and ordered, "Each of you must make me a unique piece. The goldsmith will make it out of gold, and the joiner will make it out of wood! You have a week to complete your work. I will then judge whose the best is!"

The masters went to work on their masterpieces. In a week they returned to the palace with their creations. The tsar came in and exclaimed, "So, masters, show me your talents!"

The goldsmith stepped ahead and said, "Your Majesty! Order a large tub filled with water to be brought in!" The servants carried in a big tub and filled it with water. The goldsmith untied his package, pulled out a golden duck, and put it on the water. The golden duck started swimming, quacking, and cleaning its feathers. Delighted with the duck, the whole court began clapping their hands.

The tsar exclaimed, "You've really made a wonder! I've never seen anything like it!" Then he turned round and, addressing the joiner, said, "Now, it's your turn to show me your art!"

The joiner said, "Your Majesty! Order that a window to this chamber be opened!" The servants opened the window. The

147

joiner untied his package and pulled out a wooden eagle. The wooden eagle was so skillfully cut out of wood that it was impossible to distinguish it from a living one. As soon as he turned a screw on the eagle's head, the bird rose up in the air and flew out of the tsar's chamber. When he turned the screw to the left, the eagle started rising farther up in the air. When he turned the screw to the right, the eagle started descending. The tsar, his wife, his son, and the entire court circle watched in awe.

Soon the joiner flew back to the tsar's chamber and asked the tsar, "Do you like my wooden eagle?"

"I like your eagle very much! "I've never seen anything like it! How have you managed to make it?"

The joiner began explaining to the tsar the secrets of the eagle's making. Meanwhile, the tsarevich saddled the wooden eagle, turned the screw, and flew out of the tsar's chamber through the wide window. The tsarevich waved goodbye to his parents and flew over the tsar's yard and the silver palace. Then he turned the screw to the left and the eagle flew high in the skies and disappeared behind the clouds.

The tsar was angry with the joiner and said, "Guard, seize him and throw him into the dungeon!" To the joiner he said, "If my son doesn't return I will order that you be hanged." The guard seized the joiner and threw him into the dark dungeon.

The tsarevich flew far from his native kingdom. In the evening, he reached an unknown kingdom and landed near a hut. He knocked at the door, and an old woman opened it. "Please let me stay in your hut for the night!" said the tsarevich.

"Come in!" answered the old woman. "There is enough room in my hut!"

The tsarevich disassembled the eagle, wrapped it in paper, and came into the hut. The old woman served supper. While he ate his supper, the old woman told him about the kingdom. She told him that the tsar's palace has a high tower where a beautiful maiden was locked. She was the tsar's daughter. The tower was guarded by fifty watchmen. Nobody was allowed to go into this tower. The tsar and his wife didn't want their beloved daughter to marry a young tsarevich and leave them.

"Is the tsarevna really beautiful?" asked the tsarevich.

"I don't know, my son," replied the old woman. "I haven't seen her, but people say she is the most beautiful maiden in our kingdom!"

The tsarevich wanted to look at the tsarevna. The next day he assembled the wooden eagle, mounted it, and flew to the forbidden tower. Flying up to the very top of the tower, he knocked at the window. The tsarevna was very surprised when she saw the handsome young man sitting on the wooden eagle. She opened the window, and the eagle flew into the room. The tsarevich greeted the maiden and told her about himself. They fell in love with each other, and the tsarevich proposed marriage to the maiden.

"I want to be your wife," answered the maiden. "But I am afraid my parents won't allow me to marry you!"

The wicked nanny who guarded the tsarevna overheard their conversation and reported to the tsar that a stranger had flown to the tsarevna. The tsar's servants found out that the tsarevich lived in the old woman's hut, seized him, and dragged him to the palace.

"How have you dared to break the tsar's law and enter into the tower? Tomorrow you will be put to death!" said the incensed tsar, shaking his fist at the tsarevich.

The tsar's servants threw the tsarevich into the dungeon. In the morning, the tsar, his wife, and all of the citizens of the kingdom gathered in the square to watch the tsarevich's punishment be carried out. The tsarevich mounted the scaffold and suddenly said, "Your Majesty! Can you fulfill my last wish?" The tsar wasn't happy to do it but couldn't refuse him.

"Order your servants to go to the old woman's hut and bring me my paper package!" asked the tsarevich.

The tsar's messenger ran to the old woman's hut and soon returned with the paper package. The tsarevich opened the package, pulled out the wooden eagle, got on, and flew away.

"Seize him!" cried the tsar, but the servants couldn't reach the tsarevich.

The tsarevich flew on the wooden eagle to the tower and up to the window. He took the tsarevna by the arm and offered her a seat on the eagle. The eagle carried them to tsarevich's own kingdom. The tsarevich introduced the tsarevna to his parents and told them everything that had happened to him. The tsar and his wife were so glad that they released the joiner from the dungeon. The tsar arranged a great big feast in honor of his son's marriage. All the people of the kingdom were celebrating the wedding for a month.

Snow Balls

Kids will love this delicious treat, especially during the winter holidays.

Ingredients:
1/2 cup sugar
3/4 cup nuts, finely chopped
1 cup butter, softened
2 1/4 cups all-purpose flour, sifted
1 teaspoon vanilla
1/2 teaspoon salt
Confectioner's Sugar

Method:
Mix the butter, sugar, and vanilla together thoroughly. Stir in the flour and salt. Then mix in nuts. Chill dough. Preheat oven to 325 degrees F. Roll dough into 1 inch balls and place on baking sheet. Bake for 10 to 12 minutes. While still warm, roll in confectioner's sugar. Cool. Roll in sugar again.

Tale of Two Sisters

In small village, long ago, there lived an old widow. She had one daughter of her own and a stepdaughter. Her own daughter was a mean, lazy, ugly girl. The stepdaughter was pretty; she was also a hard-working needlewoman and a fun loving person. The stepmother and her daughter couldn't stand her and made her work all the time.

One day the stepdaughter was sitting near the well, spinning. Suddenly, she dropped her spindle in the well and began to cry. The stepmother said, "You have to jump into the well and retrieve the spindle!"

The stepdaughter thought to herself, "It's better to go into the unknown than to live with my cruel relatives." She jumped into the well and found herself lying in a green meadow. The sun was shining brightly, and birds were chirping. The girl got up and went to look around the meadow.

Soon she met a herd of sheep. "Please wash us!" asked the sheep. The girl washed the sheep and continued her journey.

She walked farther and saw a herd of cows. "Milk us, please!" asked the cows. The girl milked the cows and went on her way.

She walked and walked till she saw a herd of horses. "Comb our manes and pick out the thistles," asked the horses. The girl combed the horses and kept going.

She soon came upon a hut on chicken legs. Baba Yaga was sitting near the hut. "Don't be afraid of me. Stay here and help me to keep the house tidy!" The stepdaughter agreed, and stayed with Baba Yaga. She wove, spun, cooked, and cleaned up the hut. Baba Yaga was very good to the girl and treated her with respect.

One day, the stepdaughter told Baba Yaga that she wanted to go back home. Baba Yaga awarded her with gold for her good work and presented her with a silver spindle.

On the way home, the girl met the sheep that she had washed before, and in return they awarded her with a young sheep and a ram. Then she met the cows that she had milked, and in return for her kindness they presented her with a heifer. Finally, the girl met horses that she had groomed, and in return they presented her with a foal.

The stepdaughter returned home and showed all the presents to her stepmother and stepsister. She told them about all that had happened to her. The stepmother and her daughter were very envious, and the stepsister decided to jump into the well, also.

The girl also found herself lying in the meadow. She got up and started walking. On the way to see Baba Yaga, the stepsister also met the sheep, the cows, and the horses, but she was too mean and lazy to help them.

She finally reached Baba Yaga's hut. "Hey Baba Yaga, open the door!" screamed the rude girl. Baba Yaga agreed to take in the stepsister. Because the stepsister was so lazy, none of her chores were completed. The food that she cooked was tasteless, and the hut was filthy.

Baba Yaga finally told her, "You are so lazy and no help to me. Go home! Take this wooden spindle for your bad work." On the way home, the horses, cows, and sheep pushed and kicked the stepsister. She returned home beaten black and blue and without any presents.

Pryaniki

Russian Cookies

Pryaniki are a very popular type of cookie dating back to Tsarist Russia. The name Pryaniki comes from the spicy taste and smell, which comes from the combination of ingredients. They are perfect for any occasion.

Ingredients:
1/2 pound almonds
1/2 cup water
1 1/2 cups honey
1 pound sugar
1 pound flour
1 teaspoon baking powder
Cardamom and cloves to taste
Icing:
1 1/2 pounds sugar
2 pounds chocolate powder

Method:
Dissolve sugar in water, mix with honey, and boil in a large pan. Add baking powder, cardamom, cloves, and chopped almonds. Remove from heat and add flour. Stir thoroughly and turn the dough onto a board. Roll out the dough into an even sheet 1/4 inch thick. Use cookie cutters to make various designs. Place on a baking sheet and bake in the oven for 30 to 40 minutes. For the icing, boil the sugar twice until the syrup is thick. Add the chocolate powder and stir well. Cover one side of Pryaniki with icing and let dry for 10 minutes in the oven. Then ice the other side.

Serving suggestion: Serve with tea or coffee.